how to pull girls

how to pull girls

JULIA BRUNI

Vermilion
LONDON

1 3 5 7 9 10 8 6 4 2

Copyright © 2003 Julia Bruni

First published in the United Kingdom in 2003 by Vermilion, an imprint of Ebury Press
Random House UK Ltd.
Random House
20 Vauxhall Bridge Road
London SW1V 2SA

Random House Australia (Pty) Limited
20 Alfred Street, Milsons Point, Sydney,
New South Wales 2061, Australia

Random House New Zealand Limited
18 Poland Road, Glenfield,
Auckland 10, New Zealand

Random House (Pty) Limited
Endulini, 5A Jubilee Road, Parktown 2193, South Africa

Random House UK Limited Reg. No. 954009
www.randomhouse.co.uk
Papers used by Vermilion are natural, recyclable products made
from wood grown in sustainable forests.

A CIP catalogue record is available for this book from the British Library.

ISBN: 0091891647

Designed and typeset by seagulls
Printed and bound in Great Britain by Mackays of Chatham plc, Chatham, Kent

contents

introduction

We know the story. You are a bright, cool, successful guy, with lots of friends and all that and every girl you know is trying to match you up – but something isn't working and the beautiful ladies are not submitting easily enough!

With so many beautiful and exciting girls looking for a man, why is it that eligible guys so often blow their chances? Thinking about it, blowing their chances is sometimes the better case scenario, as often guys do not even approach the girl, giving in to some last minute doubts. Yet, these are exactly the charismatic, capable, bright men that every girl wants to meet.

HOW TO PULL GIRLS

Guys, without jokes, it's time to sharpen up your act! Your reputation as capable, masculine, good-humoured heroes with romantic tendencies is at risk of becoming something of a former glory. Unquestionably, you guys want to save this reputation and avoid depriving yourselves of the company of beautiful girls. You don't want to miss all the opportunities, especially since with all the fit girls out there, those opportunities are not in short supply. On top of that, consider the predicament of those girls. Imagine the poor things, all alone, crying themselves to sleep every night because of their romance-free lives – do you want to be responsible for that?

This is not a self-help book with complex theories and psychological analysis, as it doesn't require a deep approach for a normal guy to become popular with women. This is a very practical guide, giving both Joe Bloggs and Casanovas some pointers on becoming yet more successful with girls. Every guy I know could do with some insider information or a few new pulling techniques. Whether you need to relax and set girls at ease, or to understand how girls think and what motivates them to behave as they do; or to gain competitive advantage by analysing your often mainstream tactics that are doomed to failure and develop more successful ones, or simply to iron out a few details – this book covers the pulling game from every angle. All the chapters are packed with useful tips for every stage of the women-charming mission. Here you will gain insight into what girls consider to be the essential characteristics of a desirable man. Then, of course, there is insider advice on where to actually meet the girls – guys so often get it wrong, hoping to pull in noisy bars and clubs, while overlooking the places where girls are just waiting for you. Also, here you will find the low-down on what to avoid while chatting a girl up – with the main pitfalls illustrated with real-life stories of 'losers in action' where men who are otherwise highly successful screw up big time.

The final chapters cover the whole first-date business – including how to organise it confidently; avoid blunders; recognise the places to go to and the ones to avoid; how to read her body language and use your own to make her feel more comfortable and to send out the right signals. And finally, for the first date that cools into casual friendship, here's the strategy that converts the situation into a playboy lifestyle.

Get on with it! The girls are dying to see some action.

the value of
chit-chat

This is certainly a situation that you have been in as well – you're in a bar with one of your mates. Having a drink and standing by the bar, you notice two girls sitting nearby. Your friend sees them as well and he thinks one of them is amazing. To you, as an independent observer, it's clear that the girl looks like she also fancies your friend. Now, will your friend go and ask the girl for a drink? Probably not. Why?

I've been in this situation so many times that I've stopped counting. The last time was with my friend Ross in a trendy London bar. Standing at the bar waiting for some other friends, we spotted two girls. *'That girl over there is a stunner,'* whispered Ross. *'Yep,'* I agreed. As if she could hear us, the girl looked right back at Ross, and then continued talking to her girlfriend. Ross didn't stop thinking about this girl the whole evening, continuing to mention her every now and then. Did he go and talk to her? No. He said he thought she might have a boyfriend or something. Let me get this straight for you – he is a well-educated, professionally successful man with no problems when it comes to being confident and aggressive during his business meetings. He definitely doesn't lack personality and is a very popular guy – things are never ever boring when he's around. He isn't a wimp of any kind either. So why was he unsure whether to go and talk to this girl? And why are there thousands of other guys behaving just like him?

Please, let me tell you something and do not forget it – girls want to be approached. Actually, 'want' may be a bit of an understatement. We LOVE being approached. We are dying to be approached. I'm not, of course, advocating harassment, but who doesn't enjoy the attention of the opposite sex? Doesn't it make us feel beautiful, smart, sophisticated and desirable? (Have you ever wondered why women like to go on holiday to Italy?) If you guys think that the girl will make the first move, then you're dreaming. Most girls generally still believe (and there's no indication of any developing trend away from this) that it's a guy's job to get the ball rolling. So you either do it, or she's gone.

Here comes the good news – to get talking to a girl isn't mission impossible. In fact it's not even difficult. Fine, you may be a bit nervous about approaching a girl you don't know. Maybe she won't be nice to you, or maybe she really has got a boyfriend. We're only human, and nobody likes to be rejected, for whatever reason. However, maybe she hasn't got a boyfriend, and maybe she would like one (after all, it's perfectly normal for a girl to want to have a boyfriend). She also fancies you. Yes, she noticed you there, even though she acts as if she didn't. You will be the perfect couple …. Well, only if you go and talk to her!

To begin with, you have without doubt inherited the courage and ability to pull girls. I mean, didn't your dad once have to go and talk to your mum? There you go – you were born to be successful with women. It's in your genes. All that's needed now is a strategy, and the strategy is straightforward and simple: first make all women crazy about you; then choose the one you like the best and charm her until she can't be charmed any more. Well, if you're feeling cynical then you may still be sat there thinking *'Ah, Bingo! "First make all women crazy about you." What a great idea! Inspirational, so I guess the plan will work perfectly right up to this stage.'* Now, this really isn't the challenge that you may think it is, so let's discard some myths and examine exactly what girls do go crazy for.

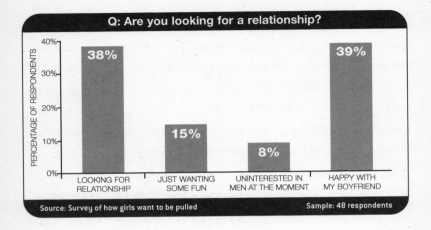

At this point it's worth dispelling the notion that most girls have a boyfriend. It may feel like this sometimes, but when we surveyed a group of girls between eighteen and thirty, we found that over half of the girls in this age range were looking for a guy (see the chart above). This, combined with the fact that over 80 per cent of single girls will accept the offer of a date if a guy makes a normal impression (see the 'Losers in Action' chapter, page 33), means that you will be highly successful if you regularly chat to girls and can come across as normal and pleasant. Can't be too hard, can it?

▶ talk to every girl

Don't forget that practice makes perfect. Start charming every woman you come into contact with, regardless of her age, appearance, the size of her boobs (or their shape) or your intentions. I mean, start talking to the opposite sex *without* any intentions. Ask the girl in the supermarket if this is the right kind of meat for a stew; ask the old grandma in your corner shop if she needs any help; and in general use

The Complete Loser's Guide to Talking to Someone
(or the elements of charm)

1. Casual smile, good eye-contact, match their body language and tone of their voice (but not too high!)

2. Appropriate introductions that set them at ease – take your time, be relaxed

3. Remember something from last encounter and ask about it

4. Find out how they are

5. Talk about what you want from them

6. Wish them the best for the day/week/year/their life

7. Say goodbye

every opportunity for conversation. This is not such an unfocussed strategy as it may at first appear. Just think about it. People don't talk to each other as much as they used to, and this is especially true when it comes to boys talking to girls. Consequently, the thought of talking to a girl must be a little scary, because it may immediately feel as if you're trying to chat her up – otherwise you wouldn't have any reason to talk to her. Which is exactly the attitude that you have to get rid of.

▶ then charm the knickers off them

The thing about women is that they love being charmed. However, men don't know this – or at least that's the impression girls are given. Remember that we are a gender of attention lovers and are easily won over by a sincere interest in our well-being. Yet men are often so functional. They ask the time, sometimes they ask directions, but hardly ever will they make the effort to ask an opinion or to give a heartfelt compliment. Guys, to be honest, girls often think that you're behaving in quite a boring way. As if it is impossible to work out that we want to hear: *'Oh, Barbara, you look stunning today,'* or *'Cindy, that dress so suits you. You look like a million dollars,'* or *'Rebecca, you looked great at the party last night!'* Let me tell you, if you say that, you will immediately become the subject of Barbara's, Cindy's and

Rebecca's fantasies (and all the women who have overheard those compliments will dream of you too!) Don't think that comments like that will be taken as sexual harassment or be something unwanted. Seriously, girls love to hear little compliments and they'll love you for giving them. And we're not talking only about young girls. Do you think that the old lady next door would hate to hear that her new hat suits her? My God, if you compliment her on anything, you'll absolutely make her day! (And it provides a useful complimenting exercise). Also, you never know – she may have a gorgeous grand-daughter who she may now want to introduce to such a lovely young man. So, get on with it!

Obviously, this does not mean the kind of inept and painful attempts to charm that result if you overdo it. Things such as calling a group of old ladies 'the girls' and similar attempts to be dashing are of course pathetic, and whoever acts like that makes a sorry impression. Oh, and the way to prove that you really like a girl's dress is not to stare forever at her boobs, trying to make her believe that you admire every stitch, you know what I mean.

Is it all that difficult? You see, we girls know that you guys are manly creatures who aren't interested in a lot of girlie small talk. And thank God you're like that, because it would be really irritating if guys

MATT THE PERFECT CHARMER

Seriously, this tactic works. Ask my friend Matt. He's the only one of my male friends who's just perfect at it. He charms girls all the time, everywhere, just like that. The following is a regular occurrence. We are out with ten guys, including Matt. They hang about drinking beer and planning the next paragliding trip or something, every now and then informing the rest that they have just spotted a tasty girl. Then they spot Matt. With a few girls, engaged in what is obviously an interesting conversation. By the time we're leaving, Matt has made an impression on the local females and they seem to be dying to meet him again – as soon as possible, judging by the clutch of new phone numbers in his possession. Now, Matt is a good-looking guy and everything, but so are all of the guys. However, he's the only one who manages to talk to girls with total ease. As we're all waiting for taxis, the other guys having failed once again to score tonight, he proves this theory right by starting to talk to some girl who's waiting in the queue in front of us. By the time she gets her cab, her number is in Matt's pocket. Oh, and he's also going with the other guys on the action holiday; he'll just help with the planning when there are no girls about.

behaved like a bunch of schoolgirls, who never shut up and are taken with everything. Surely you realise that being charming doesn't mean that you have to talk non-stop about everything in the whole world. You don't have to go on about that dress or hairstyle forever either, making it sound as if it came out of an American soap opera. But a couple of red-blooded, gentlemanly comments, or a couple of minutes of good conversation, are going to be an absolute winner. I'm telling you, the females will never leave you alone, and you are going to be the man they will dream of. Oh, and as they are busy dreaming of you, just ask them, in the middle of conversation, quite casually, if they would like to meet up for a glass of wine one day this week. It's guaranteed, the answer will be yes.

So, in conclusion, remember that it's impossible to chat anyone up without actually chatting to them! Everyone must agree with me on this. The first step to winning over the female population is to talk to them – to all of them, everywhere, without it causing cramps to either party. Then charm them with a couple of sharp compliments. Before you know it, you'll be thinking you're James Bond.

how to be
james bond

This is another very easy task. And believe me, it will pay to be as cool as James Bond. I mean, have you ever seen 007 on a desperate night out? You have to agree with me, James is The Man.

▶ how to become 007

As every guy knows, Bond never fails. Everything he does, from flying supersonic jets and jumping down high buildings to dispatching any number of the world's most dangerous villains, he does in the coolest and most astounding way, as perfectly as no one else could. There are always lots of beautiful women around who are dying to sleep with James, suggesting that his first-class skills are not limited to saving the world and his shoulders are not the only big thing about his body. The rest of his lifestyle is, of course, just as desirable. He spends his life driving the fastest cars, gambles in the most famous casinos, flies the latest models of the meanest planes and is never alone in the most luxurious hotels in the world's most exotic locations. Let's cut a long story short, Bond has got it sorted.

So it should be obvious what a guy has to do to become as cool as James. I'm sure that by searching the web (e.g. www.google.com) you'll easily find flying courses available near your home. Oh, and forget about taking it easy, becoming Bond is no walk in the park. You'll also need courses on learning to drive cars at 250 km an hour, jumping from the roofs of high buildings and in perfecting deadly martial-arts moves (unless you're already familiar with how to over-power twenty men all by yourself). After you master all of these, pop into the nearest Armani's, as the activities listed form no excuse for not looking immaculate 24/7. And you'll become the most eligible man in town and all the women will be lying at your feet...

R E L A X !   S T A Y   C O O L !

Even though those sound like the perfect mixture of the SAS and Hollywood, they are not what girls care about. Let's examine what, through a woman's eyes, makes Bond so dangerously attractive.

▶ the real attraction of james bond (according to girls)

1 Bond is a very successful man with the right amount of confidence

This is an ambitious man who achieves his goals. He is hardworking and socially capable; a doer not a talker. And he never ever gives up. He is not a geeky workaholic though, he has time to work as well as play. You can't imagine 007 answering the question about what he would want to do in life by saying something like *'I just want to chill, man, ya know what I mean...'* On the other hand, even though James is a busy man, his girlfriend or wife would certainly never feel neglected as he is a romantic at heart and would always include her in his life.

That is the kind of confidence we girls want to see in guys. Nothing less and nothing more. However, plenty of men who may not be far from the 007 ideal fall down in this area. They create a bad impression by promoting themselves too much, and if you make the wrong start then she'll judge you early and you may not get the chance to make things better. True, it does require a certain amount of aggression on your part to go and talk to a girl who you fancy but don't know. But be careful not to compensate for your nerves with something arrogant like *'Oh, it's such a nuisance. I've got to go to the garage tomorrow to pick up my brand-new BMW convertible,'* or *'Let me tell you about the half-million pound deal I landed today.'* You'll put yourself straight into the over-confident category, which doesn't have too high a success rate when it comes to charming girls.

Of course, we girls like ambitious men who know what they want to achieve in life and are working towards it. Then again, we're not cold, calculating creatures, only interested in millionaires. Your sense of humour, interesting personality and genuinely good heart are the most important things for us. Having said that, we are really not attracted to lazy bums with no goals. We want a boyfriend we can be proud of, which may prove impossible if the guy talks about his future

INSIDER INFO

If you really want to impress women, learn enough about wine to navigate the wine list. Many girls love men who know their wine – it makes the guy look sophisticated and worldly.

with *'Yeah, I can't be bothered,'* or *'No, that's too much of a mission.'* What is there for a girl to admire? What would she say to her parents to put a guy like that in the best light? That you just want to chill? Everybody would immediately conclude that she is seeing the biggest loser in town. I'm afraid being that laid back simply won't work with woman's nature.

2 It's obvious to any woman that Bond is an independent guy

Can you imagine 007 depending on his mum to iron his shirts or make him breakfast in the morning? I also bet you that his kitchen isn't full of dirty dishes and he doesn't leave his underwear and smelly socks lying about. It's also likely he's a good cook.

Really guys, if you make the impression that you are dependent on your mummy, then you get zero points. And you'd be surprised how fast girls notice these things. Girls are very observant and there are things they will know about you before you order the very first glass of wine. In general, we girls are tired of the liberation movements. We don't think that the biggest mistake a woman can make is to cook dinner for her boyfriend. (Remember, if she thought there was zero chance of you becoming her boyfriend then she wouldn't go for that drink with you to begin with.) On the other hand, we don't anticipate being exiled to the kitchen once we get married, becoming the sole executor of the boring household tasks that men can no longer be bothered with. We expect the housework to be equally shared, and we don't see much scope for compromise on this. Yes, yes, don't get your boxers in a twist. I know that you're not getting married yet. You're interested in meeting some attractive girls and maybe even doing some naughty things with them. This is just to let you know how a woman's mind works. And it's not a secret that girls usually take relationships more seriously than guys. So, yes, the idea of what kind of husband you could possibly make has probably crossed her mind for a moment. It's in a woman's nature. (I hope that the ultra feminists won't crucify me for this).

Don't get me wrong here. I'm not suggesting that you should immediately become an overly domesticated character, obsessed with dusting every day, and taking pride in never having a watermark left on your bathroom tap in order to be sexy. But a guy who doesn't know how to iron his shirt, takes his washing home once a week and eats mostly in McDonald's looks like somebody who still needs looking after.

You see, though we girls no longer consider ourselves the weaker sex, we still like our men to be strong. Your strength and independence is a very important part of your sex appeal. We're dreaming of

**The Complete Loser's Guide to
Sharing Public Spaces with Women**

1. Stop, get eye contact with the woman. Smiling is obligatory, talk is optional

2. Resist all temptation to cut in front of her, force her to wait for you to pass by or let the door slam in her face

3. Hold the door for her, let her enter a room first, and keep out the way until she passes

4. Make sure your loser friends follow your lead

capable, independent, masculine males. And masculine but incapable isn't enough. Or would you consider Homer Simpson sexy?

3 Bond is smart as fcuk

James Bond never mouths off about anything – about his achievements, his job, his possessions or his successes with women. The guy really means business. He does not give / take / talk any nonsense, and he never humiliates or slags anyone off to impress a woman.

See, big mouths are never popular with girls. Talk that is bigger than actions is a sure recipe for disaster in this game. Bond knows what he's doing when he plays down all his achievements and, as you can see, it works perfectly. If you do the same, women won't be able to resist you, because it will immediately trigger their interest in you. On the contrary, guys who talk all the time about how cool they are, simply annoy everyone and their unwilling audience just can't wait for them to shut up and get lost. Or just as bad, if you exaggerate what you have got or what you do – you know the stories of guys telling girls how they've got this cool sports car and then it turns out they've got an old banger. Make no mistake, there is nothing wrong with an old car, but the right thing here is to say that you've got an old car, it's nothing breathtaking, but it's OK – and you've just scored as many points as possible with her.

Let me tell you something about girls. You don't have to take their breath away for them to like you. So play 007's game – take their breath away exactly by not trying to take their breath away. It always works.

4 James is the perfect mix of masculinity and romance

For every woman, 007 is the ultimate hero. He is always there if a lady needs assistance and, of course, he always knows exactly what to do.

In his presence a woman has a feeling of total security. He is the most exciting companion, and he never says anything pathetic or embarrassing. Of course, even though he's the toughest, most fearless guy, he's a romantic at heart who makes his lady feel like a princess.

It has been mentioned already that women really like strong, masculine men, because we feel like we can rely on these guys to get things under control. We like the feeling of security some men provide. Just as 007 saves us from disaster in the movies, what we want from you guys is for you to be willing to stand up for us should we get into trouble. In practice, this means performing modest, gentlemanly tasks like walking us home at night.

To be as charming as Bond shouldn't be a problem for you either. We women just want to be admired a little bit and listened to; and please don't forget about the compliments either (tips on successful complimenting are in the next chapter). Unfortunately, lots of guys seem to think that to be charming means making tired old jokes about all women belonging in the kitchen and so on. (Avoid these, really, they don't tease or amuse anyone. Everyone has heard them a thousand times before, they are not funny any more, and guys are not considered to be the brightest stars in the sky for not managing to come out with anything better.)

BUT! An ego the size of 007's would never work with women in the real world. The following chapter lists a number of turn-offs for women, and Bond's obvious innuendoes are one of them. In a bar on a Saturday night, tell the girls you meet, with the utmost coolness, that you're just there for the birds and you'll soon see that those 'birds' will no doubt be caught by another animal. So beware!

INSIDER INFO

You know, we girls don't need to be spoiled rotten, but sometimes we like it if guys make a fuss of us. What this often means to guys is a bunch of flowers purchased at a petrol station, wrapped in hideous printed cellophane, still smelling of petrol and life-threatening if someone smokes near them. (Guys, never ever buy flowers at a petrol station or you'll see tears, I promise you.) To make a little fuss of girls is really easy – hold her coat when she wants to put it on; if you are both smokers light her ciggies instead of just passing her the lighter. It doesn't require anything breathtaking, just be a gentleman (to all women, not just the one you fancy). The girls will love you.

by way of a short recap:

1. Girls love successful hard working guys, who are adequately confident
2. Your independence is an absolute must
3. Overrating your achievements will not get you anywhere
4. Tell us we are beautiful every now and then

And that's about it!

Your masculinity, sexiness and attractiveness is now utterly proved. You're just the perfect male and we dream of meeting such a man soon. We girls don't care if you drive amazing cars, fly planes and can beat up lots of people. Tales of some world-saving missions just make us smile sympathetically. Well, you know, honey, men will sometimes be like little boys, and we shouldn't spoil your fun, should we.

You see, girls are not as materialistic as you may think. Obviously everyone likes beautifully designed sports cars, and I'm not trying to suggest that girls are unable to recognise the difference between a Porsche and a Lada. However, the car a guy has doesn't make the girls mad about him. The rest, the planes and stuff, is too far-fetched and unrealistic for girls to be even slightly interested in. (No sentimental childhood memories either. The girls used to play with dollies.)

▶ the douglas factor

So how exactly did Michael Douglas manage to seduce Catherine Zeta-Jones? You may say that the guy is seriously rich and famous, but let me tell you, that alone wouldn't have been enough. There must have been something else that got her hooked. As the gorgeous Mrs Douglas continues to shine with happiness, I think we can safely conclude that Mr Douglas most certainly seems to have made it. The question which remains is, of course, how did he do it? What exactly is the Douglas magic formula and has it been patented? How do you make sexy younger women crazy about you? Do you think it's impossible? Nothing is impossible!

Note: The text below isn't to be skipped by younger guys, who will certainly find a few useful tips in here as well.

why do some women prefer older men?

a) 'Old school' behaviour

Many females love the classier, more sophisticated attitude to life and to women especially. Older men aren't so casual with women – they 'treat a woman like a lady'; behave far more gentlemanly than younger guys; are more appreciative, attentive and certainly don't forget to pay compliments. I mean, guys, COMPLIMENTS! You guys don't seem to appreciate how important they are to women. Who could be surprised that the beautiful young girl goes for someone almost twice your age when the younger guys make unsolicited compliments at the rate of one every three years!

b) They find older men more physically attractive

Obviously physical attractiveness is subjective. But while we can generalise and say that there is something attractive about everyone, one thing is true – yes, some girls do find a few wrinkles and some grey hair very sexy!

c) Girls like older men because they know what they want

This ranges from being able to decide where they would like to take their date tonight to knowing generally what kind of woman they want and being able to act accordingly. Older guys don't tend to be time wasters and are capable of making snap decisions – making a very attractive alternative to the younger guys who can't be bothered, are often not sure about this thing and the next thing and who need time to 'find themselves'.

d) Life experience

Some girls like guys who have already lived a little. They like the wisdom of an older guy. These girls also argue that the guy's life experience goes hand in hand with the man being more confident and easy going.

what is the best thing an older man can do to maximise his chances?

Just be chilled and normal – for a girl who is into older men, it is perfectly sufficient that he doesn't live an 'overly settled' lifestyle, complete with telly and slippers; but is active, interested, outgoing and sociable.

what is the worst thing an older man can do?

To put it bluntly, the most unappealing thing an older man can do in order to impress the ladies is trying to act like a twenty-year-old. The girls know you aren't twenty. If they wanted someone of that age, they'd go out with your son. They like a man to be honest about who he is, and they aren't impressed when the guy who's supposed to be sophisticated runs around nightclubs intended for people half his age; or dresses like a fashion victim; or supplements his everyday vocabulary with a bit of clubland patois. As one girl put it, 'when you can smell the desperation a mile away.'

▶ the younger guy scenario

There may be times when you'll be heading for a girl who's older than you. You may be the seventeen-year-old trying his luck with the twenty-four-year-old girl you met at your cousin's wedding. Or the recent graduate trying to seduce the chairman's sexy secretary. Or it may be the relatively frequent scenario of fancying some girl and then finding out that she's actually a few years older than you. All in all, the older girl is often a very appealing option. She's grown out of the teenage blues. She's confident, chilled and at ease with herself. A zit on her nose doesn't mean the end of the world to her. She dresses sexily and tends to make fewer fashion faux pas than younger girls. And, the very best news – she's probably more realistic, tolerant and easy going when it comes to men. Older girls don't tend to be drama queens and they aren't likely to become unstable if your romance comes to an abrupt end.

so, what works with them?

It can be quite easy to pull a girl who's a few years older, as long as you don't behave like a teenager. Drop your youthful enthusiasm, stop trying to be wacky, don't use 'cool' to describe everything under the sun and don't say 'man' or some similar youth parlance three times in every sentence. Stop eyeing up and commenting on every girl around. No, I'm not saying you should become boring and miserable. Just make sure you don't come over like an excited puppy unless all you're looking for is a pat on the head.

Direct your enthusiasm on her, the older girls are interested. All it takes is for you to come over as someone who could without any problem hold a conversation with her friends. One thing is for sure – she would certainly not be wasting her time on a guy who would embarrass her as soon as he opens his mouth.

GIRL PROFILE #1: ALISON

Job: IT specialist
Age: 25
Home: Wales

What kind of guy are you looking for?
Someone who shares the same values – probably from a similar background, and with a similar attitude to life. Looks are quite important, but I would be very happy with someone who has average looks and a compatible sense of humour. While I admire ambition and drive, this shouldn't come at the expense of the guy being caring and trustworthy.

What is the problem with the guys that you meet?
They are often very arrogant and keen to talk about themselves, and don't pause to ask for my thoughts. To me, this is a sign that they don't want to get to know me – they only want a physical relationship. If guys would take more time to find out about me, ask interesting questions and avoid talking to my chest, then I would be much happier to chat to them.

GIRL PROFILE #1: ALISON

If you want a boyfriend, how do you go about getting one?

I generally believe that you meet nice guys when you least expect it. So, I don't have a specific strategy for meeting blokes – rather I get involved in sports and hobbies that I enjoy and that would appeal to the kind of guys that I'm looking for. However, it's through friends that I'd be most likely to look for guys.

If a guy fancies you, what should he do?

The most important thing is that he should be polite. I feel that he should also be willing to break the ice by talking for a few minutes, rather than putting me on the spot before I feel comfortable. Finally, if it isn't working out then he should recognise this and let me go, rather than trying to pursue me for the rest of the evening. If he's polite and charming but we're not a great match, then there's no reason why we shouldn't meet up later as friends.

What is a guaranteed turn-off?

Being tight with money is an immediate turn-off – guys should at least be chivalrous on the first date!

What has been your worst / best date?

Not really sure – although the worst ones tend to be where the guy hasn't planned what he'd like to do on the date. 'What would you like to do?' followed by 'I don't mind, what would you like?' and a long walk in the rain to find a restaurant that is fully booked is a hopeless start to a date. I would much rather the guy say 'I hope you like Italian, because I've booked us a table for eight – although this can be cancelled if you hate it!'

losers
in action

Approaching girls and charming them may not always feel like a straightforward matter. It's not surprising therefore that these ventures every now and then – actually quite often – end up being unsuccessful. The following is the result of a great deal of brainstorming and countless personal experiences. The tactics detailed in this chapter must be forever excluded from your attempts to approach and charm women if you want your mission to be successful.

When approaching girls, it's always worth remembering that most don't need to be blown away by something amazing to agree to go for a drink – the main priority is to avoid making a bad first

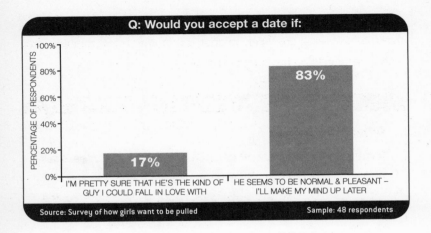

impression. When we surveyed a group of girls to find out what would tempt them into a first date, 83 per cent said they'd accept if *'he seemed to be normal and pleasant'*. My god! How hard can that be? With this in mind, the rest of the chapter is dedicated to the common techniques that are often employed by men, but which almost always spell failure.

▶ 1 vulgar behaviour

Never do things like putting your hands on an unfamiliar girl's hips or any other part of her body (regardless of how much you like the shape). You may mean it only as an innocent joke, but it's very likely that the girl will be absolutely infuriated that after a few minutes' chat a stranger thinks he has a right to paw her.

HOW TO COMPLIMENT SUCCESSFULLY

Great move ...

If you want to compliment her, and this is a brilliant idea, start by complimenting her on neutral things – if she chooses the wine, tell her it was a very good choice; if she chose the venue, tell her it's a fine place and you think she has chosen well. Show interest in the place she came from, the school she went to and things like that – she'll take that as a compliment as well. Also, you're assured of success when complimenting her on things which she obviously wants to be noticed – e.g. if she has got an extravagant, unusual handbag, piece of jewellery, scarf etc. Doing that, you are giving her two impressions of yourself – first, that you're a guy capable of compliments, which is what every woman is dying for; secondly, that you're smarter than most other males because most guys are just totally hopeless and they would never notice these things to begin with.

The same is true when you make a compliment. If you say that she's got good legs, or a great figure, or anything directly relating to her body, then she will not be at all impressed. Don't forget that you're not talking to one of your mates here. You are now talking

HOW TO COMPLIMENT SUCCESSFULLY

... but get it right

However, remember when complimenting, it's essential you are genuine. No false, overexcited comments will ever create anything positive for you. One or two remarks about you liking her dress will make her very happy; a ten-minute speech about how well this dress fits, enquiry about where she bought it from and who helped her to choose it would backfire horrendously. She would know that you don't mean it and girls know that guys don't often notice these things – therefore something is wrong here (i.e. with you). Don't overdo it when it comes to the quantity of the things you compliment her on either. One or two short compliments are an absolute hit. Twenty compliments on everything she does, wears and owns would be as painful as five big haemorrhoids, trust me.

> **INSIDER INFO**
>
> Lots of girls really are into their handbags, and they say that handbags portray character. Therefore, if you notice the handbag, the girl will somehow understand it as if you really understand and appreciate certain aspects of her personality – don't worry if this doesn't make any sense to you. It's a girl thing.

to, not about, the girl you're interested in, so making the best impression is a must. Sexually provocative comments are poison when you don't know the girl and are a guaranteed turn off. If you persist, you'll get some harsh responses, but in all honesty, you asked for it.

▶ 2 arrogance

Watch out! Many points have been lost due to arrogant behaviour. Even though it may require a certain amount of male aggression to approach a girl, take good care that you don't come across like an overconfident prat.

We girls aren't interested in guys who come over with an attitude of the main hero. The 'I-know-I'm-supercool' approach will not make us fall dead on the floor through pride and astonishment that such a superman is talking to us. Instead of being charmed to death, we're likely to take the mick out of you and make a couple of unflattering comments once you leave (often on the disparity in size between a man's ego and his genitalia).

▶ 3 failed attempts at romance

Remember, lots of things which are romantic when you are in a relationship come across as wet and desperate when you don't really know the girl.

Guys often make mistakes here in the genuine belief that this is the way that women want men to behave. True, the message shouted at guys everywhere is that they should be more romantic. Women write articles about it and are often heard talking about how they dream of a romantic guy and complaining about their unromantic boyfriends and husbands. This often seems to confuse proper red-blooded, masculine types into believing that the only guaranteed way to impress a girl is to be Mr Romantic. Then they get it all wrong once again. And they resort to sad gestures like writing a poem to the girl sitting at the next table at the café about her beauty and how her, sitting in this café this afternoon had made an eternal impact on his life. They bring huge bouquets of flowers and cuddly toys to first dates and talk about deep emotions...

Guys! The girls were talking about the attractiveness and desirability of romantic gestures from their boyfriends and husbands, not from a guy they've just met. Yes, girls love it when men are romantic, and, as was mentioned before, 007 is also romantic. But when a complete stranger writes a poem to a girl, she thinks *'My God, this is really embarrassing. What shall I do now? What shall I say to this guy? How pathetic! He wrote me a poem and I don't even know him. And I don't want to get to know him either now, when it's obvious that he's such an unmanly softie. My God, no normal guy would ever do anything like this. Besides, honey, you aren't exactly Pushkin! Well, I think I will act as if it's very nice, as he may not be all right in the head and it's unwise to make disturbed people angry... Then I'll get out of here ASAP.'*

▶ 4 desperate tactics

If you want to be successful on the pull, you have to appear to be a cool character who likes girls, appreciates their beauty and enjoys their company. But, and this is important, as much as you like girls, and maybe you especially like this one girl you're chatting up, you still have

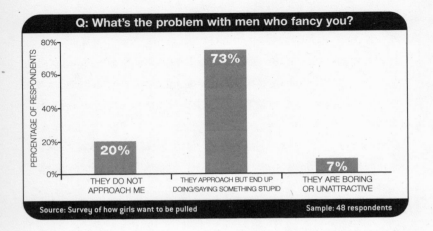

to be an independent, confident guy who has things under control. You ask a pretty girl out and accept her answer whatever it is. If she says no, don't resort to any desperate gestures or tactics. It really is outrageous what guys will sometimes do when they fancy a girl without realising that their actions are absolutely shocking and are certain to get them nowhere.

Another guy I know wasn't taking 'No' for an answer, and he got down on his knees in front of a girl to persuade her to give him her phone number. This kind of thing really doesn't work. In this case, all he got was a piece of chewing gum stuck to his trousers. These are not medieval times. Princes no longer kneel in front of princesses. You aren't going to be perceived as an incurable romantic either. Don't go on your knees or do things like that in front of girls that you don't know. It really isn't at all appealing to see a guy humiliate himself. Even though these strategies aren't the biggest shockers, it's very unlikely that they'll be successful.

The conclusion is surely obvious. Desperate tricks and tactics make you look like a desperate individual, and desperate individuals aren't at all attractive. In order for the girls to want you, you have to be the cool, independent guy who's very much in control. Of course you enjoy girls' company, but that doesn't mean that you should leave the girls thinking that a date with them is a matter of life and death for you, and if they say no then you'll never get over it. We don't want to get close to the guy who nags and pleads, making us think *'Well, what should I do now? If I don't give him my number, he's not going to be able to bear the psychological trauma.'*

Don't forget, we girls like strong, red-blooded creatures who can inspire respect. With a guy like that, we feel flattered that he has asked us out for a drink.

SHOCKING, BUT TRUE!

I know guys who have completely misunderstood the rules of the game. A friend of mine's action is a perfect example. He fancied a girl for some time. He never went to talk to her, introduce himself, make small chat or invite her for coffee. He happened to see her every now and then, without ever talking to her. However, he really went out of his way to go to places where he thought she might turn up. As he didn't know her, he started to make all sorts of assumptions about her – what her personality was like, what her job was, what she liked and didn't like and what she wanted to achieve in life. It was absolutely forever before he went up to her to inform her of his existence. By then, he felt like it was really important that this girl should like him and go on a date with him. Somehow he felt that he knew her already. So, he went to talk to her and asked her a straight and honest question, whether she wanted to go out with him. See, he thought of himself as a doer, not a talker, and she would surely appreciate a no-nonsense guy who didn't like wasting time. Therefore, he went for the closed question – efficiency, you see, no small talk, no mucking about. Give me the result here and now, luv. He must have thought his frankness would be

> ## SHOCKING, BUT TRUE!
>
> truly seductive... This girl said No. That really surprised my friend and as he'd fancied her for so long, he wasn't going to give up just like that. He told her, and this was in a café, that he really wanted to go out with her, and therefore, he'd go down on his hands and knees and meow like a cat until she said yes. He thought that this was a good way to prove to her that he's a man who knew what he wanted and was accustomed to getting it, not a loser who gave up easily. As a man has to do what a man has to do, he really went down on his hands and knees and meowed like a cat. Unfortunately, this didn't continue until she agreed to go on a date, rather the poor girl asked the chef and the waiter for help, and my dearest friend got kicked out of the place.

▶ 5 persistence

It is guaranteed, persistence will get you nowhere. Girls aren't usually that specific about the characteristics that a guy must possess in order to be eligible. The chances are they'll give you a chance at first and make their mind up about you gradually. BUT if the girl doesn't want to give you her phone number, and she's already told you in a polite way that she's not looking for a date, or doesn't want a lift or for you to walk her to the train station, then she's already made her mind up – the answer is 'No', so don't try to win her over. She'll not be persuaded and the more that you try, the more adamant she'll become.

Have you, or some other guy you know, ever tried to get a number from a girl who didn't appear to be interested, pressed on regardless and eventually succeeded? And when he tried to phone her, he found out that the number did not exist? Yep, there's no two ways about it, she didn't forget her own number, and she didn't unintentionally confuse it either. But what choice did you leave her? It's unbelievably annoying when guys are so persistent. Giving a false phone number is one of the easiest and fastest (and most often used) escape routes. Don't push her into this. A guy who nags is the ultimate turn-off. No means No. Wish her a pleasant evening and remember there are plenty of other girls.

▶ 6 chatting up girls while drunk

OH MY LORD! Let me tell you something. In this situation you aren't chatting anybody up, even though you may think you are (it's just an illusion caused by too much beer). The girls aren't smiling at you either, they are taking the mick. All in all, this is a schoolboy error which an experienced charmer would never make. Immediately stop all attempts to charm the ladies, because the best thing that could possibly happen is that they simply ignore you.

Next time when you intend to pull, remember that you're a man on a mission, so be professional about it. You can match whatever the girls are drinking, so they'll get merry faster than you and it may be easier to get their phone number (but obviously don't try to trick them into drinking a lot, or they'll get drunk and won't remember you at all the next day). If they aren't drinking, it really is better to limit yourself to a couple of beers, charm the females and start drinking in your favourite quantities when they leave.

▶ 7 mad suggestions

A couple of my friends have also tried to get a date by making ridiculous suggestions like, *'Would you like to go halves on my rent?'* or *'Would you like to have my babies?'* They thought it was a really funny thing to say, and the girl would instantly like them and appreciate their 'off-the-wall' sense of humour. Of course, it didn't work. Nothing drastic occurred. They just looked like fools for a while. Hmm, these things happen ... Better be sure that your jokes are actually funny.

▶ 8 talking about money

Don't talk about your financial situation to a girl who you don't know and have only just started a conversation with. This may sound obvious, but for some reason guys often talk about this subject, creating an awkward situation and leaving the girl just one option – to end the conversation ASAP. Once, for example, I went for a drink with my friend Sandra. We were both single at that time, so we were open to the idea of meeting someone (well, to be completely honest, we were hoping to meet someone). This guy approached and asked if he could join us. He looked pleasant enough, so we said yes. We introduced ourselves and shortly we started to talk about our jobs. We asked him what he did and he asked if we could guess. As he looked like an office type, and was dressed in a suit, we said that he probably worked in the City. To our surprise, he said in a very confident tone, *'No, I don't work in the City. If I was working in the City, I would have lots of money. But I can assure you that I don't have lots of money.'* The fact he chose to emphasise this so strongly totally took our breath away. We didn't know what to say, apart from that we felt like telling him – listen, we don't know you at all, so why is it so important to inform us that you haven't got much money? What on earth makes you think that the first thing to say about yourself should be that you haven't got much money? Do you think that we want some of your money, or what?

Needless to say our conversation was over, and Sandra and I were pretty annoyed. To our surprise, by talking to other girlfriends of ours, we've found that this isn't such an unusual thing for a guy to say. However, none of the girls like it, and they all say it is an instant conversation killer. Obviously the opposite has the same result – you guys aren't going to be popular when you start boasting about how much money you have either. Better to avoid the topic 'money' completely for now, and leave it for a much more developed stage of a relationship.

▶ 9 desperately wanting to be original

If I tell you that a very good friend of mine's chat-up line was *'Can I touch your breast?'* would you believe me? Maybe you would, maybe not. However, he really said it – in the sincere belief that girls would find it funny, start a conversation with him instantly and that he'd pull a lot. Maybe it is even less believable that he isn't some kind of silly pervert, but a very cool guy. However, his chat-up lines sometimes seem to have come straight from *Viz*. With this introduction, you'd expect him to have the IQ of a squirrel. But he went to one of the best universities and is generally a bright guy – not some kind of academically gifted, but socially incapable person. When I asked him for an explanation for his shocking one-liners, he outlined a theory that girls today must be bored with every guy repeating more less the same thing, i.e. *'Can I invite you for drink?'* So he really believed that he must be original in order to differentiate himself from all these dull guys and their obsolete chat-up lines. But unfortunately his perception of originality included tactics such as talking about breasts! Is it necessary to emphasise that these 'original approaches' are always a dead loss? Bless him. He isn't the only guy making such mistakes.

It's actually feasible to understand the thinking behind this. Lots of girls say that they want to meet someone who is 'original' and 'different' or 'himself'. Taking the vagueness of those terms into consideration, who can be surprised that guys sometimes translate this into thinking that it's a good idea to introduce themselves with a degree of absurdity that is rarely seen outside the *Jerry Springer Show*! It's original, after all. Who can argue against that? It's being 'himself' as well. Think about it, if you are a boob man then you are being yourself (which is what girls like). Also, you are being honest with them, so they should appreciate that you're a straightforward character, and not some cold-blooded, careful manipulator trying to trick them, right? And look what happened. The silly ungrateful girls are now against him, despite all his honest and good intentions.

Well, let's get down to business now. Your originality is, of course, very important, but not right now. You've just met a girl you fancy. You don't know her and you want to get a date. Saying something mad is going to make you seem more weird than original. For the moment, forget all about trying to be yourself. In any case, you are yourself. Or do you perhaps think that there's a possibility that you could be someone else?

The best thing you can do is to rely on the old, charming, polite, ask-her-out-for-a-drink approach. It's the golden path if you want to score.

▶ what girls mean when they talk of a guy's originality

I have asked lots of my girlfriends who say that they want to go out with a 'unique' or 'original' man to explain more specifically what these terms actually mean to them (and if they mean anything at all). This is a summary of their explanations:

- He's the 'unique' person for her. There is an overall compatibility between them.

INSIDER INFO

If you are inviting a girl out on a first date, never make any suggestion that you won't wait for her if she's late.

- The 'chemistry' is there.
- You're never bored with each other and you never will be. You're an inspiration for one another. You never run out of things to say.
- There are things he says and does in his own special way, and they will always remind you of him.

Hopefully, this didn't move you to tears. My boyfriend reckons it's painfully wet, but what can I do – this is what the girls had to say about this issue. As you know, the emotional females sometimes get a bit carried away! (It's commonly understood that males are far more easy-going and the whole originality business to them means getting their hands on a big pair of wobblies). However, the good news is that you don't have to worry about this in the short term. As you can see, apart from being a bit girlie, this whole 'originality' business is really geared to long-term relationships, and has got hardly anything to do with chatting girls up.

▶ 10 talking only about yourself

It's a frequent mistake that guys will sometimes get carried away with talking only about themselves. Again, it may be unintentional. Perhaps they start a conversation by saying something like *'I love this music. It reminds me of when I was in South America,'* which would be fine; but then continue with a long story about their journeys in South America, and what they did there, and how they liked it. Every now and then the girl may ask a question relating to this, and the guy goes on and on and on...

When this continues for a little too long, the girl, who didn't get a chance to talk about herself or what she likes at all, concludes that even though this is an interesting guy, who's been around the world and has got lots of good stories, he probably is only interested in himself. And she doesn't really want to see him again. Be careful that you don't repeat this mistake, because it's very likely that not all guys who do that are selfish at all. It may easily be that they were not completely sure exactly what to talk about on a first date. They were happy that they'd found an interesting subject that wasn't too personal for when you do not really know the girl. You are after all looking for something relatively neutral to talk about. Also, he may have thought that she looked interested in the conversation. She never said she wasn't enjoying it. Guys, don't expect girls to drop hints, or express their displeasure. She would have if she was your girlfriend, but she's not and she isn't going to lecture a stranger on how to behave. So don't forget that the conversation must be a dialogue and give the girl space to talk on whatever subject you discuss.

GIRL PROFILE #2: VICTORIA

Job: Lawyer
Age: 30
Home: Manchester

What kind of guy are you looking for?

I want an easy-going, relaxed guy. Sense of humour is a must. I like people who can laugh at themselves. Independence is a very important trait for me – I want a guy who wants to do his own things as well, instead of concentrating exclusively on 'being a couple'.

What is the problem with the guys that you meet?

Guys are often a bit too inactive for my liking – i.e. when it comes to things I would like to do, places I would like to go to – it's too much effort, too inconvenient, too far. Lazy guys are just not for me. I like a busy lifestyle and I'm not going to be content with sitting at home watching TV every night.

GIRL PROFILE #2: VICTORIA

If you want a boyfriend, how do you go about getting one?

Recommendations only! I'm not into dating strangers I meet by chance. I like meeting guys through friends.

What is a guaranteed turn off?

Guys with too much self-importance – I just haven't got time for this. Second biggest one is stinginess – I'm a very generous person, but on a first date I don't want us to be like two accountants, working out who pays for what.

If a guy fancies you, what should he do?

Nothing breathtaking or extraordinary is necessary. I want someone bright, pleasant and basically normal. However, when someone wants to invite me for a date, I want them to have something to say, rather than sitting there, expecting me to keep the conversation going.

What has been your worst / best date?

A football match definitely was the worst one – too much beer, too crowded, too much noise. I love football, but it just isn't a first date environment. Nothing can beat an evening in a nice bar or a cosy restaurant – for me anyway.

how to make the most of every location

Are you happy with how often you've managed to pull in a night-club? Or a bar? All right, maybe you're more of a daytime man – are your café results satisfactory? What about the girls on the train when you go to see your parents – any success? If your friends keep telling you that these are not 'the' places to chat up attractive girls, then don't listen to them! Most places and occasions have some potential if you know how to manipulate the environment to your advantage. Sometimes the situation is so favourable that not much work's required of you. But, far more often, the odds seem to be against you and the situation looks rather hopeless – and this is when most guys just give up. Yes, they fancy the girl, absolutely. But the strategies that they can think of look doubtful and the guys aren't going to risk making fools of themselves. With no winning strategy in mind, the guys decide to give it a miss… DON'T!!

This chapter presents some very cool analyses of the 'core' pulling environments, plus plenty of useful strategies and tips that will help you win the girl.

▶ good pulling environment

- ✔ It should have a relaxed feel, be unisex and offer lots of opportunities for conversation.
- ✔ There should be a high likelihood of meeting people your own age, with some similarities to you, giving you a choice of conversation topics.
- ✔ You are likely to meet single girls here and have the opportunity to talk to them for as long as you like.

▶ bad pulling environment

- ✘ There's a low chance of meeting girls your age with similar interests. If you're not likely to meet anybody you have something in common with, you won't have anything to talk about and it will be difficult to start a conversation.

✗ Places that are too busy or loud, where it's impossible to have conversation and most of the people are drunk are definitely bad.

✗ Avoid boring places that are too quiet, where there's nothing interesting going on – the girls will just want to leave.

✗ Don't go to a place with a reputation for being a meat market. The girls aren't going to trust you.

▶ bars

Generally bars are a trendy, exciting environment, where guys often intend to pull and the girls hope to meet some cool guy. But then somehow the whole situation in most bars is just not right. In some places you have lots of nice fit girls chatting together, interested in meeting guys, but the men don't appear. Other bars are full of guys, but there are few single pretty girls. Or sometimes there are lots of both cool girls and guys, but there's no interaction.

In essence, there are bars that are pulling-friendly and there are pulling-unfriendly bars, such as traditional pubs and small fashionable bars:

traditional pubs

As the key to success is to be in the right place at the right time, and you want to pull fit girls, you have to go where they go. If this sounds very obvious and logical, then why do guys who want to pull hang about in that kind of traditional, loud, dark, masculine, mostly beer-serving bars, where there are hardly any girls to be found? (Don't you realise that if they aren't there, you can't pull them, or what?) The few girls who are there aren't there to pull, believe me. They probably came there with their boyfriends, or with a closed group of people or something of that nature. But they won't go there for a drink with a girlfriend, and won't be open to the possibility of meeting a guy, because these very masculine places feel a bit rough to feminine tastes. Please, don't get me wrong. This isn't at all meant as a criticism of your favourite pub. Just bear in mind that from the pulling point of view these places aren't very useful.

small fashionable bars

The kind of fashionable, unisex, very busy small bar that doesn't have many tables and chairs doesn't offer big chances either. The attractive girls you're interested in will come here, but this isn't the kind of place they will stay in for too long. In contrast to guys, who are usually content with standing at the bar, drinking and chatting to their mates for the whole evening, girls like the comfort of sitting down at a table if they're staying for a couple of hours. As these small bars don't usually have tables available, the girls are not going to stay there for long. Also, these places don't have the chilled feel that is necessary for a relaxed conversation. They're more full of adrenaline – efficient places for whatever the specific purpose of you being there. These are exactly the kind of places, where the girls will turn up for one quick drink with their friend on the way from work or simply for something short and scheduled. As the girls came here for a specific reason, like to meet a friend, they only plan to stay about an hour or so, and they aren't going to be interested in meeting new people. These really are the cool trendy places, where no interaction between guys and girls happens.

pulling friendly bars

These are the bars where the girls go WITH their girlfriends (can you see, your options are increasing already). They come to have a long, relaxed, fun evening and share a few bottles of wine. The single girls are perfectly open to the possibility of meeting friendly guys and giving them their phone number. Unfortunately, as so few guys come to these places, this great opportunity is rarely exploited.

Do you know a modern, large bar that plays cool music, has enough tables to sit down at, is cosy, chilled, has a comfortable feel, isn't rough at all, and offers a good selection of wine? Yes, it's the one you don't really go to, because it's too feminine for your macho taste and habits. Guess what, this is the place with real pulling potential. This is where the girls go. Just have a look inside! The girls are there. They are enjoying each other's company, but lots of them are thinking *'Would the good Lord please be so kind as to send some nice, bright, heterosexual men over here?'* As this kind of guy is nowhere to be seen, heard, smelled or touched, this remains, far too often, only unfulfilled wishful thinking. The girls leave, wondering what on earth is going on. Have all the capable guys left town forever?

To anybody who is a doer, not a talker, it must now be obvious where a man has to go if a man wants to pull. Don't let your friends discourage you by opinions that these girlie places are a bit wet and stuff like that. It's not of utmost importance either, that the choice of beer in these bars may be limited and you personally aren't a wine person. Do you want to get the women or not? Remember, you're a man with an objective, so don't behave like an amateur. There may be another reason why guys don't really go to these bars – guys can sometimes be, ehem, a bit wimpy. They may feel a bit uncomfortable with the idea of trying to pull in places like that, because they think that everyone can see them, and in the event their mission happens to be unsuccessful, everyone in there will take the mick.

Really, I know what you're thinking. Life isn't fair. Why can't these silly women come to the place YOU think is cool? What is this irrational female obsession with all these modern bars anyway? The girls these days have got no appreciation of traditional values! It would be much more fun to pull in beery bars. And the females should drink beer. Apparently it makes their boobs grow. Any potential misunderstanding could be easily avoided, as all your friends would agree in advance which one has the best bum, legs or boobs, so nobody would later think you'd made some less then perfect choice. And if she isn't sufficiently swept off her feet, you'll have no problem convincing your mates that she was a lesbian. Or frigid. Or a frigid lesbian. Or, it may be, that the men do not know how exactly to pull in this environment in the first place (he he, see, I got you.) Do me a favour, don't be such a weenie. Girls don't fall for the kaka-pant types, you know what I mean. James wouldn't be scared either.

INSIDER INFO

Don't use the worlds 'tits' or 'breasts' when chatting to girls you fancy and who you don't know well. To girls 'tits' sounds too vulgar, 'breasts' too medical. Use 'boobs' instead (but anyway remember they're not a great topic for a first conversation).

HOW TO PULL GIRLS

There's no reason why you should feel less then one hundred per cent confident in this kind of bar. Pulling in here is really easy and your chance of scoring is likely to be well above average. This is due to several factors. The first one has been mentioned already – this is where the girls want to meet you. When they say that a bar is an ideal place to meet some cool guy, they mean THIS kind of bar. These places offer, according to girls, a more civilised environment than the traditional smoky, beer-drenched pub, and they will quickly draw the conclusion that you personally are also a lot smarter then the average pub character. In these 'girlie' bars people don't really get too drunk, so by meeting you there the girl will also think that you aren't the heavy-drinking type, as obviously no girl is interested in the heavy-drinking type. Cut the long reasoning short, simply by being in a place like that you have made a good impression on the girls already.

And the rest is as easy as this: you look out for the attractive females and choose the one you like the most. If you can see her and she can see you from your table, then smile at her every now and then and see if she smiles back at you. Watch her body language (see chapter 8). Does she fancy you? If she does, get your friend and go together and ask, in a friendly way, if you can join them. Then be pleasant,

HOW TO PULL A GIRL WHO IS WITH A FRIEND

This strategy comes from a friend of mine – and he swears that this is a winner. It's really useful in any location when you fancy one of two girls who are together, but you have no friends with you to help out.

Now, maybe you've already noticed that the girl who you fancy seems to have more guys after her than her friend does. This may be for various reasons, e.g. she may be prettier, blonder or whatever. The usual scenario is that the girl who has all the guys after her is fed up with it and wants to be left alone. Her friend isn't too happy either, as she's very likely to feel short of male attention. So, what does the smart guy do? Yes, you're right. He starts talking to the one who's feeling neglected. She is, of course, happy about this and is likely to be interested in continuing the conversation. At the same time, the more popular friend invariably feels curious as to why this guy isn't after her like everyone else. She'll attempt to take a more active part in the conversation, but you play it cool and don't be too keen. If she contributes to the discussion you're having, then acknowledge that and appreciate her points, but continue talking mostly to the other girl. Only later on, start talking properly to the one you've been interested in the whole time. The result is guaranteed, says Dan.

Note: it works with more than two girls as well.

charming, remember the 007 attitude (as described in the previous chapters), and you are home free. If she doesn't smile back at you, or doesn't look interested, have another look around you, find another fit girl and repeat the process.

If you fancy a girl who can't see you from where she's sitting, find some reason to walk past her. It doesn't matter what – go to the bar to order a drink, or pretend to go out to make a phone call or something. As you are passing, smile at her ... You know the rest.

▶ pulling in nightclubs
(or how to become the nightclub maestro)

Have you ever wondered what you do wrong when it comes to chatting up girls in a club? After all, the odds would seem to be in your favour. Nightclubs are the places where all the cool people go. Surely lots of them are single and interested in meeting somebody. There are lots of girls, so the chances are high you'll meet someone you like. Everybody is dressed to kill. The girls all have their make-up on, suggesting that they're interested in meeting guys. It's a long evening, so you'll have enough time to chat to them and charm them. Overall, things are looking pretty good. It should be the perfect hunting ground. So you get a group of your friends together and off you go. It's a great club, full of fit girls. You have fun with your mates, but surprise, surprise – you somehow didn't get the chance to charm a girl, let alone a couple of them. When the next time is the same, and the third, you start to wonder what's going on here, and maybe you conclude that, for whatever reason, nightclubs are actually not places where you can pull. You don't know exactly why, because at first it looked very promising, but somehow it fell flat, even though you did your best. Your mates aren't having much luck either, so it can't just be your fault. Perhaps the feng-shui wasn't right.

You'll be pleased to hear that a solution to this has been found, and we've got it here for you. We'll tell you how the clubs really work, and what the girls expect and want when they're out clubbing. And we'll also tell you what you guys do wrong, and introduce the winning manoevres (yes, they exist). So next time you're in a club, you'll be well ahead of the curve and it will be you who wins the girls.

To begin with, let's compare the girls' and guys' nights out. You'll see that there's actually plenty of difference between the girls and the guys in terms of what they are interested in and all the practical aspects of clubbing. You'll see how these can be best used to your advantage.

the guys' night out

When guys go out, especially clubbing, they generally seem to be in an adventurous mood, not too concerned about details or practicalities. Knowing that this is going to be a long night, they don't plan to leave the place before the whole thing finishes (which is usually at about 3 am). Their plan for the night is to have a laugh with their mates, drink lots of beer, meet some fit girls and chat them up. They're not at all concerned about the practical aspects of, for example, getting home. They just deal with these issues as they go.

As this is going to be a long night, they intend to take it easy. They go to the bar and start to have a few beers while they're talking to their mates. And they drink and chat, and drink and chat and time goes on and on, and suddenly it's midnight. So they decide to have a last drink and after that they want to go and find some attractive girls. After the last round, the ones who want to pull get together and go to 'have a boogie' in the vicinity of the pretty girls they saw earlier. They go and dance a bit, and find out, quite quickly, that the pretty girls they saw aren't here any more. There aren't really a lot of girls here at all now. The ones who are here are not their types or they're here with a boyfriend or for some other reason they're not the girls they want to target. Something didn't quite work out. The guys all agree the situation's lame and head back to their mates, have something more to drink and head off for a kebab before going home.

the girls' night out

A girls' night out is totally different. When girls go out, they want to have a bit of a chat, a couple of drinks, meet some interesting guys and maybe meet them again if they get on. But unlike the guys, who are relaxed about the details, a girl usually has an exact plan for getting home; which may mean leaving with her friends or even catching the last train home. Whatever her plans are, she is unlikely to drop them with zero notice. Most girls are simply not comfortable with unexpectedly trying to work out how to get home in the middle of the night. So, do not assume that the girl you fancy will still be there when you finally feel ready to go and chat to her. And anyway, when it gets towards the end of the evening your chances are very slim. Several guys may have tried to chat her up already. Maybe some of these guys were drunk. So she's likely to be fed up with male attention by now and may not want to talk to you because she suspects you're another pest. She may think that you probably have a couple of phone numbers from tonight already in your pocket, and now that the girl you chatted up earlier has left, you're trying your luck again (that is if she is even bothered to think about it). In any case, as it's getting late, she's tired and she's probably thinking of leaving soon. She may just want to finish her last drink and is not interested in meeting anybody tonight anymore, or starting any conversation. But, as I said before, the likelihood is that most of the fit girls aren't going to hang about that late anyway. And the disco divas who've stayed very late have got other reasons for being there – maybe they're really keen on the music they play. Whatever the reason is, it's not likely that they're waiting for you.

the winning strategy

As said above, the fit girls aren't going to hang about forever in a club. The best thing you can do is talk to them early – as soon as you walk

INSIDER INFO

Avoid talking about conspiracy theories or the paranormal when trying to chat a girl up. A good friend of mine tends to come out with some strange theories about aliens, for example. Though these topics may perhaps be inspiring to a different audience or situation, a girl you don't know will most likely conclude that you're a bit of a weirdo.

in. Girls are generally quite careful when it comes to giving their numbers to guys who they meet in nightclubs, because these are reputed to be the places where guys go when they want to get laid that night. The longer you wait, the higher the probability that you'll be put into this category. The conditions are also most favourable early on – the music isn't too loud yet and the place isn't so busy that it's almost impossible to move. You'll score big time by introducing yourself early, because the other guys (your competitors) will make the old mistake of hanging about with their friends first. Don't you be such an amateur. The situation is just perfect if you know what to do.

The girls want some male attention NOW and all the guys are at the bar, working up the courage to talk to a girl, or forever deciding which one they fancy most. So don't waste your time; start as soon as you can. The girls will love it, because the message you're sending out is that you've noticed how attractive they are and that you prefer their company to rounds of drinks. Also, and this is important, at the start of the evening you're going to be sober, therefore charming the female population here isn't going to be a problem. As girls are really not interested in drunken losers (who'll come to annoy them later on), they'll remember you as the best, most capable guy there. If they give you their phone number, then they will really want to see you when you phone them. This is important because lots of girls will give you their phone number in a club, but when you phone them you'll find they're not interested in talking, let alone seeing you again. They've realised after the club that they actually didn't like you that much. (They just gave you their number on the spur of the moment and now they know that they shouldn't have). Another advantage of making an early start is that if by chance the first girl isn't interested in being chatted up by anyone, you'll still have the whole evening and all the other girls there to choose from. That won't be the case if you leave it to the last moment. Also, as the evening progresses, the environment in the club changes. People talk less and dance more. The music gets louder, making it virtually impossible to hear a word anyone is saying, let alone conduct a memorable conversation. That's another reason why people nearly always fail to pull towards the end of the night. If you have to repeat your name three times before it has been heard properly, even the smallest talk becomes technically impossible. Just as impossible as trying to chat somebody up without talking to them.

So, really, get on the job immediately. They say that good things come to those who wait, but this is an exception. The pretty girls won't wait, so you don't want to wait either. While the other guys muck about until midnight and then try to get their act together, you make sure that by eleven the number of the girl you fancy is in your pocket.

▶ house parties

This really is the easy one. House parties offer some of the best opportunities and have all the characteristics of a good pulling environment. The main problem with house parties is that there are never enough of them. Most people only get invited to one occasionally. So, don't wait for other people, have one yourself. Throw house parties often. Invite lots of your friends and let them bring their friends. You're going to meet lots of new people, and they'll invite you to their parties when they have one. House parties are very easy to organise and don't cost a fortune, so it's really a mystery why there are so few of them.

As house parties are so good, there are not many tips needed here – just watch that you don't get stuck with people out of politeness. By the time you're free to chat to the two attractive girls you've been flirting with the whole time, they're leaving to catch the last train home. It's not necessary to develop tactics for difficult party scenarios, such as when the party is a bit dead – just go and find the most interesting room in the house. There's always something interesting going on in the kitchen. Just don't forget to knock on the door first, in case it's something very interesting going on in there...

▶ other parties

Not just house parties, but *every* other kind of party offers great pulling opportunities. Here's one pulling method that you may find handy at parties where girls are likely to hang about in groups. It's been proved to work wonders – three girls all charmed by a single guy.

It was at a birthday party this friend of mine went to. He spotted a really attractive girl and decided that he definitely had to do something about it. Soon he noticed that she wasn't alone, but that she had two girlfriends, and they were keeping her mum company (her mum didn't have that much in common with the other guests, who were all much younger). Suddenly, these three girls left, possibly for the ladies (girls tend to go to the toilet together, usually to talk about men). Being a connoisseur of women's nature, this friend of mine immediately went to talk to the mum, who was obviously grateful to him for keeping her company. And of course, he continued doing that until the girls reappeared. What can I tell you! They thought he was just the best – the most amazing man in the whole world. He was clearly such a gentleman, not like the other guys, but the exception, the ideal every woman dreams of. Keeping a mum company, obviously with the purest, unselfish intentions – do you know what I mean! Every girl in the world will fall for that. Note: In the absence of her mother, you should be keen to spot other people who might normally feel left out at a party for your age group – such as a granny, an old aunt or a little kid. If this seems a little unethical, then remember – sometimes the ends justify the means, and if the situation requires exploiting someone's Grandma, then go for it.

▶ daytime opportunities

Don't limit yourself pulling-wise to evenings. The daytime is just as good, maybe even better. Girls aren't really expecting guys to try to pull them in the day, which means girls are much more relaxed, natural and trusting.

Here are a couple of tricks that you may find useful for different places in the day:

cafés

To begin with, this location is usually pretty good – a café is generally a pleasant place, where girls go to spend some time, no stress or hurry. You're in the right mood; they're in the right mood. All good so far. It makes a good impression as well – girls like guys who go to a café sometimes, as cafes are civilised places and guys found in them are perceived to be sophisticated. (Oohh, cafés, darling. How very Parisian.) However, that's normally as far as it goes. Yes, it's not a problem for you to get into a café. Here you are. Yes, you see the fit girls, and they smile at you. You aren't leaving and they aren't leaving yet either. But the thing is how will you approach them? What is there to talk about? You can ask about something relating to the food or drinks there, but this won't get you very far. Consequently, scoring in a café doesn't happen very often. I mean, hardly ever.

Don't despair, and don't give up on cafés either. Here are a couple of good tactics to employ if you want to get results:

1 If you fancy the waitress – as you may well do, because lots of waitresses are nice, fit, young girls – this is relatively easy, because you'll get into contact with her anyway, through ordering food etc. Make sure you're charming and confident. Look into her eyes, ask for her recommendation, be complimentary about the place and food. You have to be very pleasant all the time. Keep smiling as she passes by, as the only time you can ask her out is when you're leaving. By then, you'll have an idea whether she likes you: Does she smile back at you? Does she look at you when she passes your table?

2 If you fancy a girl who's a customer, then nothing is lost, don't worry. Can you think of somebody – your sister, a colleague, a second cousin, a friend, whoever – who has a baby and you may have a reason to buy the baby present? Forget about asking your mum to get it. This is a perfect opportunity to chat up the girls. No, this is not the biggest nonsense ever, and if you try it, you'll see. Get a catalogue with some baby stuff in and when you're in a café start to go through it. When you see a fit girl, go to her and ask her if she could please help you for a while because you have to get a present for a colleague's baby but you know nothing about babies or baby presents, and would she please help you as you think girls will have a much better idea (if you do not know of any baby, a toddler will do). Make no mistake, I'm not at all suggesting that you should make an impression as an oversensitive, feminine softie (ooohhh, babies, ooh, aren't they cute? – NO! Nothing like that). You're precisely who you are – a masculine character faced with having to buy a baby present, got it? Let me tell you, girls love babies, they love shopping, and they'll love you as well. Oh my God, what a guy! He wants to buy a baby present. How amazing! Obviously he's too red-blooded to know anything about it. My god, this is the most amazing guy in the whole world! She now has to get a date with you, because not one friend of hers has got such a perfect boyfriend, and she can already see the girls staring at her with the greatest envy that it was her who was lucky enough to meet a guy like this. Believe me, you will have won her a thousand times over. The rest will be a piece of your favourite cake. Order her another coffee while you're searching through the catalogue, get chatting – yes, tomorrow night she's free and available if you want to take her for a drink.

shops

Are you one of the millions of men who hate shopping? Is shopping the ultimate torture for you, an absolute waste of time, and would you do anything to avoid it? And when you absolutely have to go to the shops, do you never meet any sexy girls, let alone talk to them, and is the experience just as bad as you expected, or worse? THEN YOU DO NOT KNOW WHERE TO SHOP!

Believe me, trust me, you can meet the fittest girls while shopping, and charm them easily. You just have to know how, and where to go. That's not to say that you're incapable or anything like that. But it's a sure thing that all males could do with some advice here, as they really don't seem to know much about pulling while shopping (no experience is gained through inaction, you see). To begin with, you need a woman (your mum, sister, granny, cousin) who you'll need a present for in the future. Got somebody? Great. Forget about ordering it online, or asking a friend to buy something.

Girlie Present Needed = Opportunity To Charm Fit Girls

Store this equation in a safe corner of your long-term memory. Now, how to go about it:

1 Think vaguely about what you want to buy – something where a girl's advice will be helpful. Good ideas are a handbag, beach bag, sarong, purse, scarf, make-up case or manicure kit (no perfumes, make-up or clothes – too personal, you should know exactly what you want in these instances or not buy anything at all).

2 Then, and this is very important, ask the girls you know (colleagues, friends, cousins, sisters) where they would go to buy these things. You'll immediately see that they suggest places you've never been to and probably never heard of. The efficient department stores like Marks and Spencer may offer good-value, durable, quality goods which will look new for years, but who cares? This isn't about the shopping as such at the moment. This is about using shopping as an opportunity to meet girls, with the stuff you buy being really just a by-product of this venture. And believe it, it's virtually impossible to pull in those immense shopping complexes. What you want are the places guys don't really know about, and where men are almost never seen – the trendy small boutiques, where girls hang about, a no rush, no stress kind of feel. In these boutiques, you'll be surprised how many pretty girls are around, and chatting them up isn't going to be a problem.

When you walk in, look confident but a little bit lost (macho-man-in-a-boutique expression, you know what I mean. Don't worry about practising it in front of a mirror – you're probably going to be genuinely confused anyway, making your appearance just superb). Again – casual smile, polite, civilised and all that, and ask them to help you here, please. You're looking for a present for your mum (sister, sister-in-law, cousin). You think maybe a handbag is a good idea. But you're a guy. You don't know anything about handbags, or girlie things in general. So would she help you to choose something? She will love it. Especially if you point out her handbag or something and say that you think she's the right person to ask for advice as you can see she's got good taste. She'll think you're a god – a caring guy who doesn't forget mum's birthday, but at the same time is too red-blooded to know what to do in a girlie shop; the perfect mix of masculinity and romance. Every girl dreams of a guy like that. (Surely you'll make the same effort when it comes to your girlfriend.) And after you get the handbag or whatever, it's really easy to tell her how much you appreciated her help. You'd never have had a clue yourself, so can you now invite her for a coffee or a glass of wine to say thank you? That done, you're an absolute Prince Charming, the girls are crazy about you, and 007 is the guy over there, the one all green with envy.

Attention! When you ask about the boutiques, also ask about the prices as well, just in case you don't fancy spending five hundred pounds on a Vivienne Westwood. Don't worry, there are lots of boutiques for every price range, so something reasonable isn't going to be a problem, and the cafes and bars are never far away.

▶ planes, trains – more great opportunities

One of the most unbelievable stories I've heard is the one about how my friend Senzo's parents met. It was few years ago, when his mum (who's Japanese) was on a long bus journey somewhere in the UK.

HOW TO PULL GIRLS

Among her fellow passengers were three guys who started to laugh at her, because of her oriental looks, which they considered 'funny'. Then another guy, who obviously didn't like the way these thugs were treating this young lady, got up and had a fight with all three of them. Of course, then the police got involved, ruined this romantic venture and all four guys were taken to a police station. On top of that, the one taking her side, despite all his bravery, ended up in prison for a couple of days. This is the way the ungrateful world treats its heroes... However, that's not the end of the story, because the young Japanese lady came to visit him in prison, fell in love, they got married and had my friend Senzo, whose middle name translates as 'The World Conqueror' (but who is not even remotely interested in conquering the world and his ultimate dream is to become a potter in some small Japanese village near mountains).

The moral of this story is obvious. No, don't beat people up on a bus in order to get a girlfriend, but bear in mind that planes, trains and buses provide you with valuable pulling opportunities, and you should make the most of each of them. So, there you are – on the usual mission to identify the fittest girls and charm them as perfectly as nobody else could.

charming girls on a plane

This is a great opportunity which mustn't be underestimated. You must do your very best (tactics described below) to be sat down next to a pretty girl, because after that the rest is likely to be easier than you'd dare imagine. Bear in mind that most people are nervous to some degree when they're on a plane. And this is no less true for girls. The worst moments for bad fliers are during take-off, turbulence and landing. Then you've got wimps such as myself, who are nervous the whole flight about almost everything. I constantly check the wings aren't breaking in half and every time a plane goes through the clouds, I am worried that it may be on fire. See, the thing is, as the less confident fliers are getting on the plane, they know that they're going to be nervous, so they're anxious to sit down next to somebody they can talk to in order to get through these tense moments. And, of course, we don't want to be next to someone looking even more timid than we are (this is one of these moments when a hero with things under control comes very handy – chapter 2, remember?). What we need is somebody who looks sufficiently calm and rational about the whole matter, and who can transfer a bit of his confidence to us. And that person is you.

As some contact between your neighbour and you is guaranteed, you have to do all you can to sit next to a fit girl. A safe bet is to follow the recommendation of a friend of mine who's had a long career in the airline industry: to begin with, don't turn up as one of the last people to board the plane, otherwise there won't be two seats available that are next to each other. Then, if you see some fit girl in the queue, get behind her and when you get to the check-in desk, after she's gone, ask if you could get a seat next to the girl who was there in front of you, because you've been talking together already. There are no rules regarding seating people (apart from unattended children), so it's entirely up to the staff to decide.

Obviously, if you give the impression that you want to harass every girl on board, then tough luck. But according to this friend of mine, if you appear to be a nice, normal person, the staff will grant your wish (when you find your seat next to hers – it is a great start – smile and say confidently – Hello again! How are you?). Or, when they ask where you'd like to sit it may be worth joking, *'Next to some pretty girls please.'* It's a cheesy line, and you may be punished with sixteen hours next to four screaming children. But on the other hand, this might appeal to their sense of fun, and when you board the plane you may find that they've tried their hand at some airport matchmaking. Of course, if the airline leaves it up to passengers to find their own seats, don't think twice – go straight for a pretty girl.

After you get into your seat, go to your reading or whatever you've got with you. It may still be quite a while before the plane starts to move, and it's better if the girl doesn't think that you're so eager to talk to her, that you're giving her hassle as soon as she sits down. When the plane starts to taxi, bear in mind that she might be nervous, so make a couple of jokes or chat to relieve her stress a bit (nothing unusual about it – if you look around, you'll see that everyone talks to their neighbours). And take it from there. Get the conversation going – where is she going? How long for? It's so easy. Don't forget, she may be just moving into your town and very keen on making new friends, meeting new people, getting a new man. Make sure that the conversation is really good for the last hour of the flight, because you want to meet up with her for a drink soon, and there will be no obvious reason for doing that if the conversation gets a bit boring during the time that you were together. Again, be friendly, polite (you know the routine) and get the phone number and a date.

charming the girls on a train

To start with, here you have more control over where you want to sit and, obviously, being sat next to a pretty girl is the main aim. Have you ever noticed the difference between men and women when it comes to the seating arrangements on a train? The girls aren't usually even slightly interested in running all the way down the platform, because they're wearing high heels, have one bag too many or an open can of coke – or maybe it's just for no reason at all. They tend to go into the first carriage that isn't completely full. Logically, one would expect the guys who are interested in pulling to follow the girls and sit in the same carriage. Well, does that happen? No, it doesn't. As soon as the gates open, the guys start racing towards the last carriage at the very end of the platform, because they expect to find more empty seats there. Well, there may be seats, but are there girls? Once again, you're on the pull. You have to be professional about it. Follow the girls! Believe me, you really can't pull them in their absence (unless perhaps you're psychic or something).

Right, now you're sitting next to a pretty girl – what's next? What usually happens, is that even if a guy sits next to a pretty girl, he has absolutely no results at the end of the journey. This is because he didn't really know what to talk about, or how to go about it. (Actually, that may be the reason why men don't make more effort to sit next to a girl in the first place – yes, I could sit next to her, but that doesn't really get me anywhere.)

Try this – soon after you sit down, make some small talk, just enough to break the ice, so it won't feel awkward when you look at her or she looks at you – small talk like asking where she's going (which will also give you an idea about how much time you have). Tell her where you're going, and what you're going to do there. Then stop chatting and get back to your newspaper, laptop or whatever you've got with you. Actually, don't be afraid to be the one who finishes the conversation now, even if you feel that she'd like to talk a bit more. If you do that you've made it – now it's her who wants to talk to you. Anyway, you get on with your stuff and when you get up to fetch a coffee from the restaurant carriage, ask her if she'd also like a drink. If she does, bring it for her, but don't let her pay for it – she'll offer the money, but you smile and say, *'Oh, don't worry about it, it's noth-ing.'* And go back to your reading. The girl is now dying to talk to you, and she doesn't understand why you aren't like the other guys. Don't you fancy her? Guys are normally very keen to talk to her, in fact so keen that they sometimes become pests, who want to chat to her all the time until it gets a bit much and they really start getting on her nerves. Why are you not interested? What's going on here?

And, this is exactly what you wanted. Now, close the paper and chat to her for the rest of the journey and as you'll obviously not finish the conversation, give her your number and get hers, so you can meet up later on in the week for a glass of wine.

▶ 'holiday' scenario

So, how was your holiday? What about the ladies in that exotic location, any results? One thing I know for sure is that every single guy wants to pull on holiday. It just completes the whole holiday experience – the girls all love you, your mates think you're The Man and you return home armed with the confidence of recent conquests.

So what does it take to earn some points from the foreign ladies? Holiday success obviously depends greatly on where you go, but wherever you go, you'll have to plan your strategy (unless you're going for the Ibiza holiday orgy, obviously.) Pulling on holiday is a great topic that could easily fill up another book, but in short: you have a very good chance of becoming the subject of lots of attention (if you play your cards right). Always be really friendly with everyone – and 'everyone' doesn't mean just the fit girls you fancy. Make sure you are friendly with the guys as well, because they have to be on your side. If they slag you off in their language (without you having a clue what they're saying) then you don't stand a chance. Get on well with them and they'll soon invite you for drinks where there are girls to meet. Get a holiday phrase book and ask the locals for good expressions to use. Really make an effort to adjust to the local lifestyle. People always appreciate it when foreigners try to speak the native language no matter how unsuccessful the attempt. And try the traditional foods. As always, avoid behaving in a way all girls hate (see chapter 3)!

There are massive differences in how to approach girls in different countries, depending on all sorts of cultural factors. You must consider how local guys try to pull (when do their tactics work and which merely irritate the girls), family and social structures and local taboos. Europe is a great example, with very provincial places, where the locals aren't accustomed to frequent interaction with foreigners. Here you may have to win some trust and rely on the local guys to introduce you to some girls. While the girls are likely to be interested in meeting new people, they may be easily intimidated by outsiders. On the other hand, you have cosmopolitan cities in Europe where most inhabitants daily meet people from different cultures. But then again, on a more personal level, people in cities often interact less with each other, and you must overcome a gulf of indifference if you're to impress the girls you fancy.

What you need to do is to look at the environment the girls live in and work with it. What are the local girls and guys like? For example, there are regions (particularly northern Scandinavia apparently) where the girls are reputed to be very direct – the local guys aren't that up front, so it's the girls who do the chasing. Just imagine how they must be starving for any guy who can get his act together, is interested, is good company and pays compliments. Do that and you'll probably get three at once!

Then there are countries where the total opposite is true, particularly in Mediterranean Europe – every local guy is doing all he can to be the stallion, pestering every girl he sees. Logically, with guys like that, the girls are likely to be fed up with all the unwanted attention and would appreciate a more relaxed, chilled guy, who's a good laugh but doesn't make the overt impression of being a persistent womaniser.

GIRL PROFILE #3: RADKA

Job: Secretary
Age: 28
Home: Chicago

What kind of guy are you looking for?
An unpredictable extrovert with a good sense of humour and warm heart.

What is the problem with the guys that you meet?
I don't have a problem with the guys I meet. I just haven't found Mr Right yet. I just wish guys would actually approach girls more!

GIRL PROFILE #3: RADKA

If you want a boyfriend, how do you go about getting one?

If I fancy someone, I usually try the eye contact, body language, talking and listening to him … I don't have any specific requirements about where to meet guys … either he's pleasant enough to be worth the conversation, or he isn't – that's it, really.

If a guy fancies you, what should he do?

Just to be normal and himself is perfectly sufficient for me. We will either get on or we won't.

What is a guaranteed turn-off?

The guaranteed turn-offs for me are definitely arrogance, a big ego, over-dominance, lies, pretending that something never happened, and not leaving me certain kinds of freedom – my own space to do what I like to do … which is necessary for me. I am offering the same in return.

What has been your worst / best date?

I've never had a really bad date. I either had one or didn't. Well, maybe once. It was quite long ago. The guy invited me for a date. He was younger than me, and obviously he had some other priorities in life, because he went to a pub instead. I mean, without me. Even today, I don't know if he forgot about me or he was too thirsty.

5

why girls are rude to guys

Even though we sometimes manage to drive you mad, we girls are generally not horrible creatures. In fact most of the time, we're charming, pleasant, clever, wise, capable, funny, intelligent, understanding, easy-going darlings. Surely every guy you know will confirm this for you. Men simply adore us because we make their lives interesting, exciting and fulfilled.

But sometimes we can be rude to guys as well, that's true. However, that's not likely to happen for no reason. There are things which you guys do which we don't like and if you do it, yes, we're likely to be rude: in other words, it's once again your fault!

HOW TO PULL GIRLS

The chart below shows the results from a survey of girls where we asked them under what circumstances they would be rude to a man who approached them or asked them for a date. Even though 15 per cent of girls may be rude if they're approached when they have a boyfriend, it's easy to see that most girls aren't usually rude to guys for the fun of it. What really makes girls feel like being rude to a guy is unwanted persistence, and making her feel embarrassed is also a certain recipe for facing her wrath.

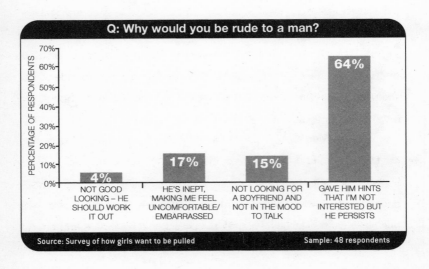

Q: Why would you be rude to a man?

Not good looking – he should work it out	He's inept, making me feel uncomfortable/embarrassed	Not looking for a boyfriend and not in the mood to talk	Gave him hints that I'm not interested but he persists
4%	17%	15%	64%

Source: Survey of how girls want to be pulled   Sample: 48 respondents

▶ if you are rude to us first

You may not realise it, but sometimes you're rude to us, so how do you expect us to behave in return? Even though amazing, we're still only human. Let me give you an example, a typical situation that you may have already experienced. As you know, plenty of girls believe in star signs. Consequently, the question *'And what star sign are you?'* may be amongst the very first a girl you've just met will ask you. You, a no-nonsense male, may consider astrology as just some silly superstition and immediately answer this poor girl by saying that you don't prac-tise mumbo-jumbo and that you can't believe she is so naïve as to fall for such trash herself. Guys! Calm down. We know that your main star sign is Testosterone. That girl was just asking an innocent question to open a conversation with a stranger. But as you've been so rude to her, she's now going to be rude to you too. You can bet on it. Sorry, you lose this time round.

▶ if you are rude to somebody else

Without being a goodie-two-shoes, women are not interested in nasty guys. And it doesn't make any difference whatsoever if this guy, who has been witnessed being horrid to someone else, is nice and charm-ing to the girl he fancies. The girl's very likely to show solidarity with the injured party and stand up for them by giving this offensive loser the brush-off. Be careful here, you may accidentally say something you didn't even mean but girls are emotional creatures capable of getting very cross very fast if they feel that some kind of injustice has been done. And this is especially true if you are rude to another girl. Female solidarity is much more developed than the superficial pretence of non-competitiveness that is the basis of male bonding. A guy who fancies a girl who's been rude to his friend is not likely to be discouraged provided that she's nice and charming to him personally, smiles at him and flirts with him a lot. Then he feels ten feet tall, believing that he is now the tiger, and sod the friends. He's the one winning the game and this competitive aspect of the male personality seems to override any sense of solidarity with his mates (you see, you men are just such traitors). A girl would never behave like that, even if you treated her as if she were a princess. I'm telling you, say something rude to or about any other girl and your princess will go off like a neutron bomb, so watch out!

▶ if you come across as arrogant

I am warning you again – females in general are allergic to arrogance. It is a hated, inexcusable trait and girls won't be interested in trying to understand the deep psychological reasons why you behave like a pompous jerk. In this case, girls will actually feel that they've an obligation to be rude. Because you are behaving like such a horrible person, you probably are a horrible person, and you should certainly not be allowed to get away with it. So there!

▶ if you are too persistent

The girl may feel that she has exhausted all the other possibilities, and being rude to you is one of the last options for getting rid of your unwanted attention. At the first suggestion that the two of you should meet up for coffee, she smiles but excuses herself, *'Maybe some other time.'* But she doesn't mean that she wants to see you another time, as she didn't say something like *'Maybe one day next week'* or anything indicating a real intention to meet up. It's not that she's an extremely indecisive person, incapable of making any plans. It means never. But she doesn't think it's necessary to spell it out for you, as she doesn't want to embarrass you and she expects that you'll get the message. In this situation, there are two good options for you to choose from:

1 Immediately accept that she doesn't want to meet up and that's the end of it.

2 Alternatively, you can offer her your phone number (once), and tell her that she can phone you sometime if she wants to. In all honesty, the chance of her phoning you isn't great, but you've offered the number, not forced her to accept it, so no points lost. (Don't be persistent about this either – if you are then she's most likely to take it to keep you quiet, and throw it into the nearest bin when you've left.) Unfortunately, lots of guys don't get the message, and when the girl tells them, *'Maybe another time,'* they lose their cool through further questions – *'That means when?' 'On the weekend?' 'What about Saturday night?' 'Oh, man! You are just not getting this, are you?'* thinks the girl, who tries to conclude the conversation with something like, *'Well, no, these days I work such long hours that it leaves me with no time at all to meet up and I'm so busy with so many other commitments.'* And she thinks, *'Now he'll get it and leave me alone.'* But, some guys don't understand even then, retaliating with something like *'....oh, do not tell me you work so hard all the time, nobody does! It's not good for you anyway, to make yourself so exhausted by work, and it is impossible that you would not find any time in your diary just for a couple of hours. Work should not be the most important thing in your life. Everyone deserves a break, so do not take your commitments too seriously!'* It's at this point

INSIDER INFO

Never, I mean never, tell a female audience that when women say no, they really mean yes. It's a painfully stupid thing to hear.

that the girl concludes she's encountered one of nature's unfortunates, who's only going to be deterred with a really harsh put-down.

There's also another kind of persistence guys sometimes employ, and that's when the girl gives them a specific reason why she doesn't want to see them: they try to invalidate her explanation. A typical example would be a situation like this: a guy invites a girl he's just met to go out for a glass of wine. She's not interested in any games and tells him honestly then and there, that's she's grateful for the invitation, but she has a boyfriend. The guy (who would obviously not like it if somebody was talking like this to a girlfriend of his) tries this pathetic tactic and says, *'Yes, but it doesn't matter, does it? This is the twenty-first century and everybody is entitled to their personal freedom. You shouldn't allow your boyfriend to be an obstruction in your life…'*

Never, never ever, do this. I can guarantee that you'll just make that girl furious. She'll think you're a stupid fool who, God alone knows why, thinks that he's got the authority to lecture her on moral values. Her boyfriend's an important person to her, otherwise she wouldn't have told you about him, and you know that as well. Even if, by some chance, they were just splitting up, you've absolutely blown it now and she's 100 per cent sure that she doesn't like you and never wants to see you again. Besides, now it doesn't take a rocket scientist to recognise that you're only looking for casual sex anyway. You're asking for an impolite answer here and you'll get it. Can you really be surprised?

▶ if you are staring at her breasts

Again, you surely didn't mean to. Or are you genuinely surprised that she noticed you staring at her boobs? You could have sworn no one could have ever noticed! (And don't stare at her bum either. She'll know. In this case telepathy works with absolute reliability.) Besides, that silly girl doesn't have to make such a big deal out of it, does she? She should understand that you're genetically programmed to do things like that. You can't help it. According to my friend Paul, it's women who should be blamed for this anyway, not the guys. Once Paul and I got into a discussion about men staring at girls' cleavages. Earlier, we were at my friend Lily's house. A friend of her brother came to visit. I promise you, that guy wasn't talking to Lily, he was talking to her breasts. He really made perfect eye contact with them and maintained it the whole way through the conversation. When the conversation was over, he said goodbye to them and left. Poor Lily! It was funny and embarrassing at the same time. However, according to Paul, guys can't be held responsible for this kind of behaviour: *'Yeah, women, first they walk around wearing a top with a cleavage so big it almost reaches their knees, push-up bra, so their breasts are absolutely everywhere. But of course, when you look, you're the biggest pervert. So why are these women showing us their breasts in the first place if they'll absolutely crucify you if you look? So why do these women do it? They show off their breasts as much as they can, but they don't want anybody to look at them, yeah, sure.'*

Guys, however much you may agree with Paul, don't stare at girls' boobs. It will really not get you anywhere. The girls will really laugh at you, believe me. Paul knows it as well. He was only taking the mick, but he knows how to behave. Otherwise he wouldn't have pulled so often. When you're talking to a woman, the perfect eye contact is to be made with her pair of EYES, OK? (But my boyfriend says that not staring doesn't mean not seeing.)

GIRL PROFILE #4: LINDSEY

Job: Student
Age: 19
Home: London

What kind of guy are you looking for?

I don't really look for a specific type of guy. I must admit, I prefer good-looking guys, although a good personality certainly shines through and makes a plain person attractive. I like a guy to be funny and reasonably talkative. Good manners are absolutely essential. If he's a good dancer and music lover it's definitely a plus for me.

What is the problem with the guys that you meet?

Most guys who try to chat me up seem to think that shocking lines such as 'What's a girl your age doing with body like that?' are a compliment. Also, lots of guys just don't get it when I'm not interested and they won't go away. Another thing I find is that most guys could do with better manners, less arrogance and less vanity.

If you want a boyfriend, how do you go about getting one?

I like the idea of having a boyfriend, but I am not interested in a serious relationship. I don't do anything specific about meeting guys – I meet

GIRL PROFILE #4: LINDSEY

them through friends, in clubs, bars. I have got a very busy social life and meeting people isn't a problem for me.

If a guy fancies you, what should he do?

Treat me like a lady, make me feel sexy, beautiful and special. Respect for me and others is an absolute must.

What is a guaranteed turn off?

Rudeness and being blind drunk.

What has been your worst / best date?

The worst one was with a guy who invited me to a very cool bar in London – but then hardly said a word the whole evening! The best one was an evening out watching the stars – very romantic.

nobody is perfect, girls included

As we've already discussed, girls are mostly nice creatures who are in general appreciative of your gentlemanly manners. However, sometimes you may (indeed you probably will) meet an exception to this rule. In the previous chapter we talked about girls being rude to guys as a response to the guy's inept behaviour, or possibly due to a misunderstanding. It was a chapter that gave the female view and explained to you guys where you make mistakes and what the reaction is likely to be so these mistakes can be avoided in future. In contrast, in this chapter we discuss the female equivalent of a male obnoxious jerk. Some girls are just not the lovely ladies that you're interested in meeting. Just as some guys are arrogant losers, some girls can be pretty unpleasant without any good reason.

There's no point in avoiding this theme, as most of the guys I know have met girls like that, but, luckily not very often – girls are quite rarely horrible without provocation. So, just be aware that one day you may get a nasty surprise.

So when are girls most likely to be unjustifiably horrible? The most common explanation must be that the girl is on a little power trip. It may be because of low self-confidence, but sometimes girls feel that they have to prove something to themselves by being rude to a civilised guy.

Richard and Oliver are the two friends of mine who've most recently come across such pathetic behaviour. They were in a bar in an industrial town, where they were visiting some family friends, and they spotted two attractive girls. The guys went over and asked them in a civilised way, if they could buy the girls a drink. The girls exchanged looks. *'Hhhmmm, they want to buy us a drink. What shall we say? Do we want them to get us a drink or not?'* one asked the other, loudly. *'Well, I'm not sure,'* was the answer, again spoken loudly. Of course, by then the guys weren't at all interested in spending any more time with these girls when they were asked,

'And what drink do you want to get for us? What shall we have, champagne?' The guys went for what was probably their best option. They said that if the girls wanted a drink, they'd get it for them, but actually they could see that they would probably prefer to be left alone, so goodbye.

Consider these as no-win situations. You've come over well and if the girls were equally well-mannered, then they wouldn't have acted in the way they had. Therefore, there's no reason for you to hang about and try to convince them of your good intentions or to make them realise they're being unfair. To analyse why they behave like that isn't a subject for this book, and it's probably not of interest anyway. You're a guy who wants to meet some nice girls who you'll like, not an unpaid psychologist or psychoanalyst. The best thing to do here is to maintain your dignity and get out of there fast, as anything else is just a waste of your time and efforts. And don't become disillusioned with the opposite sex in general, please!

Sometimes girls act in other ways that are equally unimpressive – like accepting your offer to buy them a drink or take them to dinner without having any interest in you personally, sometimes even flirting with other guys while it's you who's going to pick up the bill. Some girls will even go for a couple of dates with you, without really liking you, just because they've nothing else to do and it's better to go out with a guy then to sit at home.

So in conclusion, nobody's perfect and sometimes you'll find a female who'll act stupidly. But it really doesn't happen that often, I promise you. Anyway, now you are aware, if you weren't already, that it may happen to you one day. However, this shouldn't be the end of the world or your interest in the pulling game. Now, let's move away from these less happy topics and get back to making the moves on those who are willing to play.

guaranteed first-date success

You've been chatting up and charming every woman you meet, you've found yourself a gorgeous girl and now you've got her phone number. Full marks so far. But to score the big points you'll have to seduce her with a romantic evening that presents you at your best. The most nerve-racking part of the whole process is almost certainly that first phone call – such a simple task, yet with so much potential to screw up the whole thing! But guys, bear in mind that it's not just you who's edgy. The girls are nervous about it as well. That's why they giggle when you phone them, and consequently they feel silly about behaving like schoolgirls when you'd surely expected a far more mature attitude.

▶ making the first phone call
always phone within three days

Girls expect you to be in touch within a couple of days. If you do it later than that, without having a good reason, it's very likely that her girlfriends will have already convinced her that you tried to chat up other women in the meantime, that it didn't work out, and so now you're trying your luck with an old number (girls aren't that silly, you see). Even if that's not the case, and you've been genuinely nervous about phoning, you know that you simply cannot admit this. She'd think that you really were a wimp and there is no demand for wimps. Real men aren't afraid to phone a girl! If you have a valid reason for phoning her late (like you've been out of the country for a couple of days), tell her as soon as she picks up the phone or she may not have much interest in talking to you.

be disciplined about the phone call

Make two suggestions for a time to meet up. If she says no to both without suggesting a day when she can make it (regardless of the reason), then don't continue by offering other dates and times. Draw the subject to a close by saying, *'That's fine. When would suit you?'* She'll either give you a time, or she'll stall with something like *'I'm not sure. I'm very busy these days. Give me your phone number and I'll phone you when I can make it.'* In the latter event she probably isn't interested, but don't give up just yet. She might have genuine reasons for saying that. Maybe she really does have to work overtime for the next two weeks. In any case, now she's got your phone number, so don't phone her again as you'd look desperate. You've done enough. The ball's in her court now. If she wants to see you, she'll be in touch. Just don't make the mistake that many guys make. They phone a girl to invite her out, suggest a certain day and time and she says sorry she can't make it (fair enough, people often have all sorts of previous plans and commitments). The guy, unsure about the phone call to begin with, instead of suggesting another time, interprets this as a rejection. Worried about making a fool of himself, he decides to terminate the call with *'OK then, goodbye'* and puts the phone down. It's difficult to get the balance right between being too persistent and not giving her the opportunity to relax and agree on a time to meet. But you can't go far wrong by starting with a couple of your own suggestions and then finishing with an open-ended question that lets her think of a time if she has a hectic schedule.

get all the details you need

It can happen that a guy makes the phone call, she wants to see him, they agree on the day and the time, he says goodbye, puts the phone down and realises that they didn't arrange a place to meet. When he phones her back, he of course feels like a fool. It is really worthwhile writing down all the information you need before you dial her number. Put it aside, and when you're about to finish the conversation, have a quick glance at it to confirm that you've got all the details sorted out. Of course you'd not get things like that wrong in different circumstances, but believe me, regardless of how many degrees you possess, here you may screw up big time through nerves.

think of three good places to take her

Another frequent scenario is catastrophic indecision. A guy phones a girl to organise a date, and after getting the day and time sorted, he asks the girl, *'And where would you like to go?'* To which the girl says, *'Oh, you choose.'* The guy says, *'Oh no, it's up to you.'* And it goes on like this forever. The guy is trying to do his best to be democratic and gentlemanly. He doesn't want to come across as bossy. But the girl is thinking, *'My God, I should never have said yes. This guy just sounds so pathetically indecisive, and we're only talking about where to go for drink. We haven't even met yet and I'm bored of him already. He probably is one of these overly homely characters, who never goes anywhere. That's why he doesn't know any bar because he always sits at home. Oh no! This will be the dullest guy in the world.'* I'm not saying you should be bossy or anything like that. But a certain amount of decisiveness is absolutely essential here. You are inviting her out, so you should have a plan.

Girls are attracted to guys who know what they want. A really good move is to ask her first if there's anywhere in particular she'd like to go. If there is, then that's where you go. If she says that she doesn't have anything specific in mind, you suggest a good place which you know and ask if getting there is easy for her. Girls are not usually difficult about this, and she's unlikely to oppose your choice. But just in case, have a few alternatives ready. By the way, it's absolutely essential that you're familiar with these places, and you're sure that each provides the right environment for a first date. You really don't want to make the same old screw up as many guys, who see some bar somewhere, it looks cool from the outside, but they haven't been inside yet, and they take a girl there for a first date. She has travelled across half the town to get there, and now, as soon as you walk in there, the place is a nasty surprise. And you are facing precisely two options – either you immediately suggest another place, and the girl will think that you're a bit of a loser; or you stay there, have a bad date, and the girl will think that you're an absolute loser!

▶ tips on the venue

So, where is the best place to take her on the first date? You may be thinking, *'Should we go to a bar for a drink? Or to a restaurant? Where do girls want to go? Will she think I'm tight if I don't take her to a good restaurant?'*

I got together with lots of friends, girls and guys, and analysed this subject. The following are conclusions drawn from a wealth of experience of first dates in restaurants, bars, cinemas and every other location you could think of. These tips should really help you to make the best choice, as well as getting useful insight on the advantages and disadvantages of every type of venue.

As part of our research, we also asked girls where they'd like to go to on a first date. As can be seen from the graph opposite, the majority of girls prefer to go for a drink, although more than a third favour eating in a restaurant.

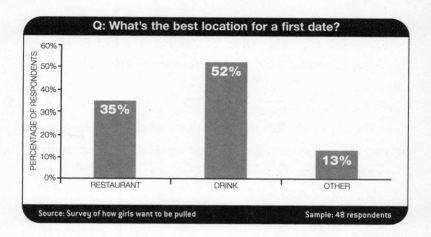

Q: What's the best location for a first date?

Source: Survey of how girls want to be pulled   Sample: 48 respondents

bars – perfect for the first date

You can't overestimate the importance of a first-date location, and a bar can provide the perfect environment. In most towns there's a large variety of good bars, meaning that everyone can choose one which provides the right atmosphere to suit the occasion. The best bars offer a casual, comfortable, vibrant environment, where it'll be easy to relax and have a long, informal, relaxed chat – which is, after all, what first dates are about. Don't worry about whether a bar is 'special' enough, imaginative enough or sufficiently impressive. You are not going to be perceived as stingy either. Remember that the girl doesn't really know you, and that by giving you her phone number she doesn't mean at all that she is hopelessly in love with you. It's much more likely that she thinks you are a cool, friendly guy, so she'll go out for a drink with you to see if you get on at all. At this stage, girls are really not interested in anything too flash. Your date doesn't want to feel guilty if you pay for something really expensive and she decides you're not her type. Don't take this as discouragement or anything like that. It's just to emphasise the casualness of this occasion.

Girls really prefer to keep the first date a low-key affair, so don't go overboard – it may make you look a bit desperate as well. One or two bottles of a nice wine (nothing too pricey) will be just perfect and are all you need for the whole evening. (As you're both likely to be a bit tense at first, you'll be grateful when the effects of a little alcohol kick in!) And also, let's be frank here, you don't want the girl to go out with you because you'll fork out for something fancy. You want her to go out with you because she likes you, right? Another thing which is a must for a first date is that you should have some degree of control over the situation. That is easily achieved in a bar. You can choose where to sit (leather sofa, or you get the table), instead of having to let somebody seat you, obviously without having any clue about your situation. These may sound like petty issues, but believe me, this kind of thing can make a big difference. You really are in charge here. If it gets too noisy, or too boring, or whatever, you finish your drink and go somewhere else. There really is no reason for getting stuck in a bar. Bars generally have a cosy atmosphere, everyone is chatting and drinking, which is exactly what you want to do, and there's no reason why you should feel uncomfortable or out of place.

restaurants

If you want to take her to a restaurant (in my opinion a bar is better, but it's your date), again, think thoroughly about every aspect of the place and about how well these fit with your plans. You can't leave a restaurant as easily as a bar, so you need to be sure that the one you've chosen is going to do the trick. Knowing the place is an absolute necessity, as there's a lot to take into consideration. Do you get on with the waiters there? Is the place too businesslike, or too intimate? A candlelit dinner is almost certainly too oppressive for a first date. But is the place too bright? Glaring lights will make you feel uncomfortable, and she may become overly conscious of her make-up. Is the place usually busy? You don't want to take your date into a nearly empty restaurant where you'll be the focus of attention. By the way, I take it that you know roughly what she likes to eat – for instance, that you are not taking her to the Gaucho Grill only to find out that she's a vegetarian, are you? The cash aspect is another detail that you should take into consideration, especially if you have something really posh in mind.

Remember that a first date doesn't guarantee you a relationship. You may not get on at all. You may find that you don't actually like her that much as a person. It's good to have found that out right at the beginning; the question is, are you happy if this discovery costs you a hundred pounds? It was even more expensive for my friend Steve, who splashed a small fortune on a first date in a chic restaurant in Chelsea. The girl turned out to be an absolute nightmare, indulging herself in the most expensive starters, aperitifs, a lobster main course, dessert and a selection of rare and outrageously priced wines. She wasn't interested in her date. She just wanted somebody to take her to a restaurant she couldn't afford herself. She sounds like an expensive nightmare, doesn't she? Oh, and Steve admitted that she was also ugly. Well, we always look on the bright side – the bill gave Steve such a cardiac workout that he didn't need to go to the gym for a week. However, this is just one of the worst case examples, so that you get that plan of taking her by helicopter to the Ritz definitely out of your head.

There's an equal chance that this date will be with the coolest girl in the world and you'll get on like a dream. So, if a restaurant is the chosen first-date venue, the recommendation is to go for one of those informal, cosy, friendly places – with the kind of feel that lots of Greek, Turkish and some Italian restaurants have. These are wonderful relaxed places with a warm atmosphere and reasonable prices. In a place like that you should also be able to choose where you want to sit, as the waiters tend to be more easy-going than the waiters in expensive restaurants.

Compare this to some of the smarter places where you'll be instructed, *'Please wait here to be seated!'* (I, personally, am allergic to this convention, as in my opinion the choice of table should be yours.) Such a place can be all so proper that you may feel like you shouldn't touch anything, everything is precise and perfect, apart from you, because the table is so full of plates and glasses and everything, you can't even move, let alone make yourself comfortable. You may be seated too far across the table from your date. And you are aware that every time the waiter comes to your table, it means an interruption in your conversation, which on the first date could have taken a bit of effort to get going, right? Yes, the silver service may be faultless and the food delicious, but does it really matter that much to you right now?

Don't get me wrong. I'm not conducting a campaign against

restaurants here. But if you choose a restaurant for a first date, then comfort and a very relaxed feel are the most important criteria.

cafés

Cafes are not the best venues for first dates. Here it's almost guaranteed that there will be no immediate results. We recommend you go for the café date only if you get the vibe that she's not up for meeting in a bar. In this situation, give her a choice with something like *'We could go to a bar for a drink sometime next week, or maybe just meet up for a coffee one day this week?'* If she goes for the coffee option, again, even though it's just a café date (and you won't be up close and personal), choose the venue carefully. Make sure that you can get a good table. You don't want to end up standing at the bar or sitting in the café's main thoroughfare (the table right next to the toilets isn't ideal either).

In general, a long-term view needs to be taken on daytime dates. Take it easy. Chat and keep her interested. Things may either develop into the bar stage quite soon, or you may continue seeing her every week or so for a coffee – in which case, give it a low priority, and date other girls, as you're just friends really. See what happens. If you two end up only as friends, think about the advantages – she'll introduce you to lots of her girlfriends.

cinemas

'Tonight I've got a date with Lisa. She's really boring, so I always take her to the cinema.' That's what one of my friends used to say (they've split up since – she really was boring, but apparently she also had the most beautiful legs, so you understand it was quite a dilemma).

Cinemas aren't only good for entertaining boring girls. They're handy if you, for whatever reason, want to test the water first. Going to a bar means it's a date, so if you're a bit unsure about inviting her for a drink, take her to the cinema. With this invitation you can keep your motives ambiguous. Even if you're a bit nervous, it's not at all difficult to start talking about a movie and then tell her that you're going to see it soon and that it would be great if she joined you. You aren't saying anything explicit, but at the same time all options are open. Obviously, go for the earlier showing, as you will want to invite her for a drink afterwards.

▶ watch out – the following may ruin your first date!

big presents

Never turn up for a first date with a big or expensive present. Girls don't want things like that on a first date. It sends out all sorts of negative messages – that you're trying too hard; that you're probably desperate; that you don't get any dates and that you'd do anything for this girl to like you; that you're trying to make her feel obliged to see you again if she accepts the gift; or that you'd like to be romantic but you got it wrong. Or, even worse, that you generally haven't got a clue.

Presents on the first date are not a bad idea *per se*, but go for something small and understated – a little bag of chocolates or a small bouquet of flowers, or something insignificant and funny.

being late

Even though girls like first dates to be casual, friendly events, take the greatest care not to be late. It really feels very embarrassing to wait for a guy. It's like a scene from some comedy, where an ugly, unpopular, desperate girl, who nobody wants to go out with, finally gets taken for a drink, and she waits and waits, as she's so grateful that a man has shown even a slight interest in her. No matter what explanation you give, turning up late always gives the message that you simply didn't care enough to turn up on time, regardless of your possible genuine reasons, or events beyond your control. So watch out! Lots of girls also have a rule about not waiting for the guy on a first date. So don't be shocked if she turns out to be one of them and leaves when you're five minutes behind schedule. It really is quite amazing that some guys are so naïve that they expect a girl to wait for them as long as half an hour! Let me tell you, if you think that, you don't know much about women. They would prefer to be seen dead rather than waiting for a guy to turn up for a first date, especially if it's somewhere where she might meet somebody she knows. (Can you imagine the embarrassment? She's waiting for you and suddenly hears, *'Oh hello. What are you doing here?' 'Ehmm, I'm waiting for my date to turn up.' 'Ooohh, dear! Don't worry about it too much, you poor thing.'* My God, guys, do you know what I mean? Waiting is really not an option for us.

Attention! This is not the case vice versa. You ARE supposed to wait in case she is late. And she may well be, because lots of girls usually are. And don't be difficult about it either, or you'll be immediately perceived as an intolerant, annoying pain in the neck who is just Wrong and should grow up. Simply put: she can do it, you can't. Don't forget that, OK? Life is not always fair and there's nothing you can do about it. (You have shorter cues for public toilets.)

being overdressed

Clothes can make a difference, so think about what you're going to wear. There's nothing to be gained from turning up dressed formally.

INSIDER INFO

I hate to tell you this, but it's better to leave your pink shirt at home this time. Lots of girls absolutely hate pink shirts on men, and in case this girl is one of them, it's definitely better to play it safe.

This is an informal occasion and you're just putting up another barrier. Overdressing can make you look like you're trying too hard, which doesn't usually work well. Also, you don't want to look like some old-fashioned chap who isn't quite with the latest trends – 'smart casual' is perfect for dating. Now, this isn't to say that you can't turn up for a date straight from work wearing a suit if that's how you dress for work. If you spend every day in a suit, you probably feel pretty relaxed and casual dressed this way. But, don't choose to dress up like that, especially not for the first date. Somehow girls can sense the difference.

being drunk

Do you think it doesn't happen? Is this so obvious that it's not even worth mentioning? Then be careful, because it happens to people like you. No, it's not necessary to lecture you on the possible consequences.

You can surely imagine them yourself. Just don't end up vomiting out of a window like my friend Joe, or like Dan, peeing out of a window at her parents' house; or Ryan, who got lucky for a change, but then threw up on her bed.

immediately accepting her offer to pay

As mentioned already, it's not at all necessary or advisable to take the girl to an expensive place in order to seem generous. But, as a general rule, wherever you end up, you should expect to pick up the bill. Girls very often offer to get the next drink or to go Dutch. Never agree to this the first time they offer, as most girls on the first date just say it in order not to appear stingy. They expect you to refuse. Lots of girls also offer to share the payment in order to test you, to see if you are the tightest penny-pincher ever. If you let her pay, don't be at all surprised if she never wants to see you again, or that there's always a shortage of girls who'll go out with you. You are the man, and you should pay the bill, end of story. This has got nothing to do with greed. Sometimes we just want guys to be gentlemen (and a few drinks never caused anyone to go bankrupt). So, as a rule, always refuse the first offer she makes. If she feels, for whatever reason, particularly strongly about paying her share and persists, then let her; but make it obvious that it's not at all what you expected and you would be quite happy to pay the bill yourself.

trying too hard to be intimate

You know this feeling on the first date. You like the girl, she's just as fit as you remember, but, now it's your first date and you're both a little tense. So, you feel that you have to do something about it pretty fast, because you really are interested, and you really want the two of you to feel relaxed as soon as possible. You want to have a laugh. You want to be on that touchy-feely, personal level. This is where lots of people screw up, ruin the whole date and that is usually the end of it with this girl. They try too hard and move too fast, become all loud even when they can see that the girl is not loud at all herself. They became all touchy, keep grabbing her hand, cracking jokes, they laugh a lot and generally become a bit hyper. DON'T!

Remember, there's an intermediate stage in this game which you simply can't skip if you want to be successful. Really, this first stage is unavoidable – instead of shouting, match the volume of her voice. Mirror her body language and, generally, the whole way in which she behaves. Don't be hyper, but be warm and friendly. Don't desperately try to be a comedian, but be pleasant, get an idea of her personality, her sense of humour. Then, after you've warmed her up, you're on the same wavelength, and she's enjoying your company, you can start to get a bit more familiar. Grab her hand when you want her undivided attention. When you say something, get a bit louder and more personal. You don't have to monitor her every move or anything like that. You'll generally get a feel from her reactions for whether she likes it or not. Of course, if you get the feel that she's getting a bit defensive, take a step back, wait for a while and then go forward again. Got it?

reading her body language

Pulling girls can be one of the easiest things in the world if you're able to understand a woman's body language and act accordingly. Through her body language, she'll subconsciously tell you when she's uncomfortable, bored, relaxed, even whether she fancies you. This is an area where men can be comparative Neanderthals – while women have a much greater fluency, subconsciously exploiting a diverse vocabulary of subtle gestures, men are too often completely oblivious to all but the most brash and obvious signs. Don't get scared though – for your purposes, you're not required to become a body-language guru. Keeping your eyes open is more or less all it takes. (As you can see, I am quite realistic about your enthusiasm to multitask.)

This chapter covers the essential body-language skills for dating, enabling you to assess her mood, empathise and to use your own gestures to slowly evolve her mood ready for a relaxed and fun date. Obviously, these techniques alone are no guarantee that the girl will find you attractive if she wouldn't otherwise. But they are perfect for putting her at ease quickly and creating a relaxed atmosphere in which she can see you at your best, while making her feel confident, sexy and charismatic.

▶ is she feeling comfortable?

As a guy, you may find the very possibility that she might not be totally at ease slightly surprising – why should *she* feel uncomfortable? Isn't it you, after all, who's supposed to take the lead on a date, organize the whole thing, make sure everything works out well, and, in short, be a superman? But there are things which make girls feel uncomfortable. She may simply feel a little nervous; or she may not like the place you take her to, but not want to tell you in case she seems like a spoiled little cow who doesn't appreciate the effort you're making. Or she may feel slightly frustrated that she doesn't have much control over something (maybe she wants to keep a certain distance but you do not seem to get it and are moving too close to her all the time). Or perhaps she doesn't agree with something you're saying but isn't aggressive enough to tell you. Please note, these are the relatively understandable reasons. Then there are other reasons – but what guy in the world would ever understand the misery caused by a bad-hair day or by that red spot which appeared on her forehead this morning? Or that she thinks that she looks fat today? As you can see, Mr Man, there's no point in analysing this. Just believe it; the girl may be feeling uncomfortable too.

how you can tell if she feels uncomfortable

The main signs are easy to spot – watch to see if she's leaning towards or shifting away from you, and if she's using anything to form a barrier between the two of you. If she feels comfortable, she'll come close and keep the space between you open. If she feels uncomfortable, she'll do the opposite: leaning away in order to maintain more distance from you (especially if you keep moving towards her), and she'll subconsciously use anything available as a barrier – for example, the glass of wine or handbag that she'll put between you and she'll keep her arms tightly crossed.

One rule to remember regarding body language is always to look at the whole picture; look out for all the signs. Drawing a conclusion about anybody's mood because of one detail that you've spotted may do more harm than good. Isolated gestures and signs can be ambiguous; they may be the result of a bad habit, or you might simply have misunderstood.

By way of example, have a look at the pictures on the next page. The woman on the **left** is the one not feeling comfortable – you can see that she's leaning away from the man. With body language generally, it's necessary to pay some attention to the details. Here, for example, she could just take a step back to maintain the distance she wants. But people don't often make such clear gestures as they don't want to look rude, and besides, it wouldn't help anyway, because the other person would most likely just take a step forward. Therefore you need to watch for more subtle gestures, such as her leaning away from you. The glass she holds in front of her is there to serve as a barrier. Of course, people normally hold glasses like this, but in this case, it will be there constantly and won't ever be held to one side or put on the table.

In contrast, the woman in the picture on the **right** feels comfortable. You can see she looks as if she's moving towards the man, and generally is moving closer to him. She's holding her glass in the same way the uncomfortable woman is holding hers, but she'll soon move it

or put it down (one example of how assessing her mood according to one isolated sign could make you draw the wrong conclusion).

Obviously, when people are sitting down much of their body language, even though communicating the same message, changes. At the same time, a lot stays the same. You can still read a great deal from the distance she puts between you, for example. The girl may still lean away from you, but now she'll be a bit restricted in her movements. Other signs to look out for are:

- **Crossed or half-crossed arms** – are just as defensive as when she's standing up, although she could just be cold.
- **Legs crossed above the knee** – are likely to mean that she's feeling uncomfortable. However, with some girls it's just the way they like to sit. If her knee is pointing towards you then this is often a courtship gesture.
- **Other barriers** – such as a drink or handbag put between you are perhaps even easier to spot sitting down than when standing up.

what is the comfortable distance?

For the purpose of approaching women, one rule which must always be obeyed is that you must not invade the girl's intimate zone. The intimate zone is the space around our bodies which we instinctively consider personal to us, and we tolerate only the people closest to us (parents, lovers, close friends) entering it. Consequently, stepping into this space of hers on a first date or when you've only just met is a recipe for failure; it guarantees that she'll feel very uncomfortable in your company. However, the issue is made complex by the fact that the size of the intimate zone varies between people. Generally, it can be from 15 to 45 cm (6 to 18 in), depending on many factors, but for our purposes it depends mostly on where she comes from. As a general rule, the size of a person's intimate zone is determined by the space they were allowed when they were growing up. People brought up in cities will have smaller intimate zones than people brought up in the countryside; Europeans will generally demand less personal space than Australians, and so on. It's perfectly feasible that your intimate zone is smaller than hers, and consequently you may invade her space without realising, so you must watch out for the signals. The woman on the **left** in the first picture (on page 133) provides a good example. She needs a zone that is bigger than the man's, but he doesn't seem to realise and keeps moving towards her. She's trying to maintain a comfortable distance by leaning away from him – and probably thinks that this slimy guy isn't worth the backache – really harsh, taking into consideration that the guy's only sin is that, being a New Yorker, he didn't realise a Shropshire girl needs more space than he does. Obviously, the situation can also be reversed – so don't jump to the conclusion that the girl from Rome you're chatting to surely wants to have sex here and now just because you, an Anglesey man, feel that she's trying to get on top of you whatever it takes! Look at the picture on the **right** on page 133. The guy here has got it right – he's given her all the space she can possibly need and now she, comfortable in his company, is coming nearer to him.

barriers

It's not only objects such as drinks and handbags that people use to form a barrier. Even more often, they'll cross their arms and legs to put up a wall. These barriers signal that a person is feeling uncomfortable and defensive. Here are three examples of body language to watch out for when trying to assess a girl's mood.

Strongly defensive (left)

Both of her arms are crossed, as are her legs. Though her legs being crossed is, on its own, an ambiguous signal (she could be cold or

desperate for the toilet), this combined with the crossed arms makes the message clear – she looks very uncomfortable.

Half-defensive (middle)

One arm is held across her chest to create a barrier and her legs are crossed at the ankles. This is a stance a girl is likely to adopt at the beginning of a first date. She isn't nearly as uncomfortable as the woman on the **left**. Her half-defensive position is likely to signal that she is just a bit cautious or nervous, which is understandable on a first date. No need to worry if you apply the right approach (you want to be warm and friendly, and you must use all the right body language – see opposite). She will relax.

Relaxed and comfortable (right)

This woman's standing straight, there's no slouching and no crossed arms or legs. This is the stance of someone who feels comfortable and confident.

▶ is she interested?

Oopps, something isn't working out! Whatever you're doing or talking about, it fails to interest her. It could be that you aren't involving her enough in the conversation or that she couldn't care less about the motorbike you've been talking about for two hours; or that your never-ending monologue on the subject of toilet fees in different countries would have left her brain-dead had she actually listened to you properly. Alternatively, the reason for her boredom may not be the actual subject of your conversation. Possibly there's something about your body language that makes her lose interest – perhaps you're too far away from her, or you're maintaining some barriers for too long. To cut short a long list of possible failings, it's sufficient to say that something in your attitude is making you seem cold or distant and she simply gave up on it. Remember that most communication is non-verbal (i.e. hand gestures, tone of voice and so on); even the most exciting stories will be dull if the non-verbal communication is poor.

How do you recognise indifference?

The following are the clues to watch out for (again, don't focus on isolated factors, but look at the bigger picture):

- **She is supporting her head with her hand** – so as to stop herself falling asleep.

- **She doesn't talk too much** – because maybe the topic doesn't really involve her and she's bored with listening to somebody else's never ending story.
- **Her eyes wander** – around the room as if she's looking for something more interesting; or perhaps she just stares right through you.

- **She slouches** – supporting her exhausted limbs on whatever she can.

It's worth noting that yawning doesn't always count as a sign of indifference – it's very likely that she's just tired and it has nothing to do with being bored.

▶ courtship gestures used by women

So we have the perfect scenario – she's relaxed and interested, and now she may be using subtle body language to indicate that she fancies you. This is what a body-language expert would refer to as 'courtship gestures'. Women have an enormous range of courtship gestures, very few of which seem to be understood by men. Some of these signals are meant to do little more than give some gentle encouragement, while others are much more assertive and unambiguous.

- **She is patting and smoothing her hair/clothes** – preening like this is a subtle way to show the man that she finds him attractive, or to draw some attention to herself.
- **Dilated pupils** – sometimes called 'bedroom eyes', when her pupils get larger, are a sign that she likes you. Although, as with

most other such signals, there's a second possibility – you're just in a dimly lit room.

- **She uses the intimate gaze** – when talking to strangers, most people look primarily into the other person's eyes or at their forehead, which is the 'formal gaze'. The first stage of intimacy is the 'social gaze', where she will look at your whole face, with her eyes flicking down to see your nose and lips. The 'intimate gaze' is somewhat more provocative, as you'll sense that she's looking you up and down – she's probably still making good eye contact, but her eyes may flick or wander occasionally, momentarily focussing on your neck, shoulders or chest. Your instinctive response will probably be to match the type of look that she gives you, but once again, don't be tempted to enforce greater intimacy by blatantly staring at her boobs!

- **She is pointing her foot towards you or positioning her body to face you** – this could just be because of the seating arrangements, but bear in mind that it could also be a courtship gesture.

- **She catches your eye, then looks quickly away** – everyone knows that this is a real sign of interest. If she does this often whilst you're talking to her, then she may be slightly in awe of you. If she does this twice from across the room, then you absolutely must go and introduce yourself!

If she's using courtship gestures, then bingo – she's giving you the green light, so go for it, the situation requires action. This is exactly where most guys just completely throw away their chance, by – God alone know why – doing nothing. It's unbelievable how often this happens: the girl is giving such obvious signals she really fancies the guy, both consciously and unintentionally she does everything anyone could think of, and the guy sits there, or stands there, like a loser, doing absolutely nothing about it. Of course, nothing will come of nothing and then there are so many guys wondering why they don't have girlfriends. This is why! Sometimes you guys really don't seem to have a clue, sorry to be so honest.

Women subconsciously use body language in quite unobvious, understated ways; so here are some practical examples to help you to identify the courting gestures:

In the **picture on the right**, you can see that she has angled her head so that her neck is exposed, a sign of trust; her legs are crossed above her knees to maximise the attractiveness of her legs (a conscious effort to make them look slimmer and more toned); her hand is on her hip – a very sexual, primal gesture, with fingers pointing to you know where!

Again in the **picture below**, you can see a combination of courting signals. Her hand is on her hip – the same, very sexual

gesture used before – and her whole body is shifted to face the man (because she finds him attractive). She's also trying to point one of her knees towards him; her legs are put into a position where they look their best. She's fondling the stem of her wine glass and exposing her wrist, so the object is held up more as a sign of trust than to create a barrier.

In the **picture on the right**, you can see a number of courting gestures. She's standing up straight to show her whole body at its best: she's preening by smoothing her hair and in doing so exposing her wrist and neck, whilst the other hand is placed on her hips, making a strong sexual gesture.

Even though it should be obvious, to avoid any misunderstanding, I must spell one thing out: even if the woman is using courtship gestures, and these may look quite sexual or have some sexual origin, it does

NOT mean that she definitely wants to have sex with you. Her body language is a collection of quite animalistic, unintentional gestures that can safely be read as saying she finds you attractive. Nothing more and nothing less. Also, these gestures do not guarantee that her interest in you will last. She may like you, so instinctively use some courtship gestures, until you, for example, come out with a confession that you don't believe in closed marriage and that you think swinging is the way forward – and for that matter, you know of a few good places to try it out which, would you believe it, could make your beauty's courtship gestures stop with neck-breaking speed.

Seeing all those encouraging signals, what does a bright guy do? He finds an acceptable way to make physical contact – briefly touching her hand, arm or knee. This is, obviously, done in a friendly, warm, spontaneous, almost non-sexual way, just as if it were only to get her full attention when reaching the punchline of a joke or to emphasize a surprising revelation within a story. Watch out! This certainly doesn't mean overtly sexual actions like stroking or massaging her thigh, unless you want to look like a sleazy desperate slimy rapist. Of course, ill-conceived romantic actions like holding her hand in a sensitive way will come across as wet and pathetic here, and you don't want to be seen as wet and pathetic, as it wouldn't make any sense. Your warm gestures will bring a warm response – she'll probably smile and laugh. It's also possible that she'll faint with happiness that in an ocean of all those incompetent geeks, there's finally one guy capable of getting his act together. When she wakes up, the first thing she'll do is phone her girlfriends to talk them out of giving up on men forever, as there may be a few more guys like you in the world.

▶ body language you should never use

Your own body language plays a great part in the non-verbal communication between you, so obviously it's important to get it right. Avoid making any intimidating or threatening gestures and communicate a message of sincerity and charm, without implying either inferiority or superiority. Here are some tips about what is cool and what is not when in a woman's company:

The **left-hand picture** on page 147 shows a seated man who conveys an impression of arrogance. His hands are held behind his head in a very dominant, authoritarian manner. His head is thrown back as if to make others feel that they are lower than he is. The whole pose suggests an unpleasant attitude and an attempt to make others feel inferior.

The body language of the man in the **right-hand picture** on page 147 is very defensive. The crossed arms make him look really uptight. Though mirroring her body language is the first step in changing her mood (see page 153), this gesture should always be avoided as it'll appear that you're cold and unfriendly.

The **picture opposite** is a better model for a 'default' pose – it is open, friendly, relaxed and allows you to turn your body towards her. Neither superiority nor inferiority is implied, and your straight back makes the best of your physique and shows confidence.

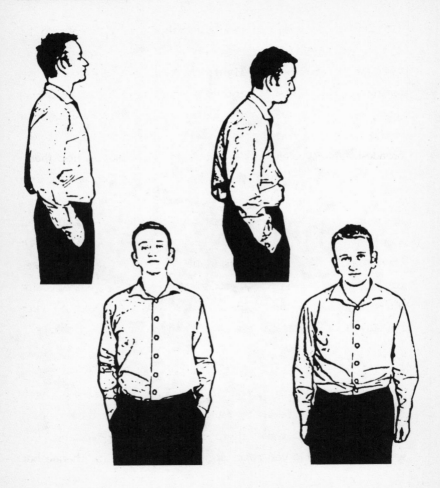

Similarly, the way you stand also makes a real difference. In the picture opposite the two images on the **left** illustrate good posture, while the two images on the **right** show how many men slouch when talking to girls. It's best to stand up straight and hold your head level (not angled too far up or down). It's a beautiful posture, making guys look attractive, open and relaxed, and your shoulders will be at their broadest. Unfortunately, lots of guys don't know how to hold themselves and, as they're taller than most of the girls they talk to, they slouch and look down, because they think that this will make the girl feel more comfortable. Guys, please stop slouching! If you want to set a girl at ease, then use open body language and a friendly smile. Of course, you may not even realise that you're slouching. But, it makes you look as if you can't be bothered to stand up properly or that you're too nervous to be an alpha-male. It's very unflattering to your physique, making you look like an old grandpa with back problems.

▶ how you can change her mood

So there you are, trying your best to charm her, and here she is, standing away from you, defensive. You wonder what on earth this woman wants and what you should do to make her more comfortable. The worst possible thing you could do is to try too hard to change her mood; for example, she stands there with her arms crossed and you try to put your arm around her in an attempt to convince her that you're a warm, friendly guy. The key is to lead her gently into feeling relaxed and fun, and hopefully, approachable.

- **Mirror her body language** – start off doing this so that she feels that you're on the same wavelength. If she stands there with her arms crossed, you cross your arms too (as shown in the **picture opposite**). If she keeps holding a wine glass in front of her to form a barrier, you do the same. Don't worry about her noticing what you're doing and seeing through it – she quite simply won't (test it with your friends first if you like). Keep mirroring her body language for however long it takes. It really will help you to build up a rapport, because it looks like you've both interpreted the environment similarly; it gives the impression that you identify with her thoughts and you're both thinking alike. This, after all, is the essence of what girls are looking for – a guy who really understands them and has the same approach to life; the person who is 'perfect for her'.

- **Slowly lead her to wherever you want her to be** – but only after you've been mirroring her body language for long enough to

win her acceptance (and give her the message that you feel the same as she does). Start by slowly unfolding your arms, go a bit nearer to her and slowly move the glass (or whatever there was to create a barrier) away. A good idea may be to show her the palm of your open hand, a gesture which conveys honesty and is an ideal start to getting her out of a defensive position. She should start to feel at ease, begin to copy your body language and really feel altogether much more comfortable (as can be seen in the **picture opposite**). This approach can be applied to most social interactions – whether you're with your friends, parents, boss or whoever – therefore, there are plenty of opportunities to practise, should you not immediately feel confident using this technique on a date. Do whatever it takes to master this, because it will help you a great deal in creating a situation where you're both comfortable. She'll feel that she doesn't often speak to a guy who understands her so well.

- **Make it sexy** – if she doesn't do it herself, get in a few cheeky jokes; maybe tease her a little with some subtle innuendo. Your gaze should be less formal and you should allow the occasional physical contact, such as briefly touching her arm or knee, to become more frequent. This stage obviously communicates a lot of attraction, so it may not be the very best idea to try it first with your mates or your boss as, one way or another, the result could be painful! Good luck. You'll have to get it right without much rehearsing. But always remember, taking it too fast will intimidate her, so if whatever you are doing doesn't seem to be completely welcome, stop, go back to the previous stage, take it easy and start again slowly when you feel the time is right.

mission accomplished

S o you've taken her out on the first date – how did it go? It's time to reflect on what you've achieved and to improve your technique for the future. In this chapter, we're going to evaluate what you've learned and how you can build on this to create even more pulling opportunities in future, even though it may for the moment look like you've just landed yourself a girlfriend. However, don't leave this chapter until after the first date, as you may need some of the following advice on the date itself.

First of all, let's get something straight – there are only two possible outcomes from your first date.

1 bingo! everything went well

So now you've got a beautiful, perfect girlfriend. Mission accomplished! Congratulations. Sounds like you are the tiger! So, tiger, you've got what you wanted, now you have to deal with it. Good luck! All females can sometimes be a nightmare, and this one managed to trap you and trick you into believing that she is some easy-going soul. Now you're a trapped tiger. Forget all the lads' nights out. Enjoy your time in captivity!

2 oops!

It is either very obvious that you two didn't get on for this or that reason, or you can just feel it anyway, even without it being spelled out. The date simply didn't work out as you had hoped it would. So, what to do now?

Obviously, your strategy and actions will depend on your particular circumstances: is it you who didn't like her that much? Or did she not seem to fancy you? What do you want now? Do you want to try to win her over, or are you not interested in her any more? Do you know why the date went badly? Or are you not sure, and would you like her to tell you? After all, it's rarely a bad idea to investigate a problem in order to avoid repeating a mistake.

In any case, don't panic or fall into despair, hit your head against the wall or jump off a bridge straight under a train; don't worry – everything is not lost.

▶ first priority

At the end of the date, just as you're saying goodbye, thank her for coming out and find something positive to say about the evening – something she said that you can enthuse about. Don't be false, don't pretend that it was the best date you've ever had and that everything was almost too exciting to bear. But, however boring or negative the date might have been, there must be something interesting, funny or useful in what she said – e.g. even if she only came out with a boring story of a boring holiday, it involved telling you how she got the £19 flight to Barcelona, which you didn't know about before and now it is certainly handy to you. Or if she told a funny story, then mention it again now and tell her how it made you laugh. You simply want to find a few words to end the date on a friendly and positive note; it really shouldn't be difficult.

This will leave the door open for you later, whatever you want to do. Remember, you've made quite a big effort so far and even though it didn't work out along the lines of your wildest dreams, don't let it all go to waste. (By now you should be a real pulling professional anyway, and professionals are efficient.) You may still be able to fix things between you and her, that is, if you're still interested. Even if you're not, you still want to be friends with her, because, bear in mind, she has got lots of friends – girlfriends. And obviously you want to meet them and pull them.

▶ you didn't like her much

As mentioned above, you still want to be friends with her. It may be the case that while you didn't find her that attractive, you think she's a good laugh and you really could be good mates. Or, even if you're not interested in being too friendly with her, you still really want to get on because you want to meet as many of her girlfriends as possible.

So keep in touch, but downgrade from what you did on the evening of your first date, so she gets the message that you're not inviting her on another date. Girls are always interested in new friendships. They want to have male friends just as much as they want to have other girls as friends. (Don't we all like to be popular?) Therefore, inviting her for a cup of coffee one day in the week, or meeting up to go to the cinema will do just perfectly to begin with. After that, invite her to your party (and obviously tell her to bring her friends with her).

She'll ask you to her parties and other dos; and before you know it, you'll have met ten girls through knowing her.

▶ you like her but suspect she is not crazy about you

Again, let me remind you, don't even dream of giving up yet. You really should eventually end up either being with this girl, or, being the ultimate Casanova, knowing most of her girlfriends (and you can bet that some of them will be pretty tasty).

So, this is what you do: you act as if you think she likes you and ask her out for another date in a friendly, understated way that puts no pressure on her. She will either say yes, let's meet up – which is obviously great – or, she may say no. That 'no' may only be alluded to. She may well go for the indirect way. Sorry, but she's very busy for the next few weeks, has too much work and commitments of all sorts. (Blah blah blah – you know the story; if she's saying all this without giving you any indication of a day when she IS free and she CAN make it, it very much means no.)

However, directly or indirectly, if she says no to a second date, you accept it. Offer to walk her home (especially if it's late), and say goodbye. Don't act desperate or be persistent. Don't try to give her some last-minute explanations or apologies. Don't try to convince her. Retain your strong independent persona, and, most importantly, don't bully her or do anything of that nature.

When the girl leaves, she'll think along the lines of – OK, it didn't go well, but he accepts that and says goodbye like a normal, civilised person, so he can't be that bad. Maybe he was just nervous and he's normally cool in a more familiar environment. Lots of nice, intelligent people sometimes act like idiots when they don't feel comfortable. Maybe this guy is actually all right and I've jumped too fast to the wrong conclusion.

She may now not be sure and may want to meet you again. Give her about a week, if she doesn't phone you (be sure she's got your number), give her a bell and invite her for a coffee or something. Again, play it down a bit now – an afternoon coffee somewhere is better than looking as if you are trying too hard by inviting her for dinner on a Saturday night.

You may get on better this time and there is still the chance of a romantic outcome. Or you will at least become friends. You never know, the latter possibility may prove to be the better one, as you may fancy a friend of hers much more.

Also, one more thing – when you meet up for the second time, ask her (pleasantly, casually and with some humour, don't be intense or too serious) what went wrong during the first date. Yes, there's a chance that she won't tell you; in that case, let it lie and don't push her. But, if she does enlighten you, it might turn out that the problem arose from a misunderstanding that you can clear up now. If you can't make amends, you may learn something useful so you don't make the same mistake with other girls.

conclusion

Everyday life, let alone special occasions, is just full of pulling opportunities. Unfortunately, it's not very often that men actually capitalise on these. Attitude is everything and the world is full of single beauties impatiently hoping that their Prince Charming will finally get his act together!

Guys, being forever single is not good for you anyway (and you know it!) Come on, what man doesn't enjoy the company of beautiful women?

This is a very short recap of how you charm them until they can't be charmed anymore:

HOW TO PULL GIRLS

1 Start off by being generally chatty to all women. Don't be an amateur – always be alert and switched on in a woman's company. Get into a conversation, show interest, pay compliments. This is what women love, but only rarely get! Don't choose one particular girl and then be really charming to her alone; make every woman feel special. Your objective is to become popular in the company of ladies in general. Women love men who are loved by other women.

2 You don't have to be Superman, a world champion or any other kind of supercool species to be successful with women. The female half of the population is fairly realistic about life and a girl will appreciate it if you don't try to take her breath away with your brilliance. We girls are fully aware and content with 007 and similar male role models living purely in the world of fiction. All that women want is a fun, bright, civilized guy who's looking to achieve something in life and who has something interesting to say, and who can make a girl feel appreciated and beautiful.

3 This is a list of 'don'ts' in women's company: don't touch or comment on any part of her body if you don't know here very well; don't be arrogant, which women hate for obvious reasons; never act